DIMENSIONS

Mysterious Triangles of the US

CHERYL LYNN CARTER

ISBN – 9798451404638

Contents

"Thank you, Cheryl Lynn Carter for this great book. After all these years, it brings back my desire to know what's really going on." - John Goulette "Fire In the Sky"

"Cheryl Lynn Carter takes us to a place of high strangeness in visiting the mysterious 'triangles' of the United States. These are bizarre places where people sometimes seemingly vanish without a trace. Cheryl presents us with not only the history surrounding these locations, but the chilling details of what exactly has occurred within them. While reading this I found myself looking into the sky in search of UFOs who might be coming to abduct me. The thought of vanishing without a trace is quite terrifying, especially hearing about it in concentrated areas like these triangles." - Alex Bobulinski

"Renowned author and researcher Cheryl Lynn Carter takes us on a quest to unravel the mysteries of different dimensions of time that exist. What are they and what really happens? Can we really move through time and different dimensions of the universe? Can we move backwards or forwards through time and space or do we just disappear into another realm all together?" - Dawn Pierce

Foreword

Lake Michigan is a bewitching body of water. Not only has it long been a means of travel, shipping, and entertainment, it has a mysterious side, as well.

If you're sitting in the sunshine on the top deck of the car ferry that shuttles you across the lake between Muskegon and Milwaukee, mobile phone in one hand to monitor your location and hot dog in the other from the vendor on the crowded passenger level, you feel so entertained and connected with the world that you might as well be at an amusement park.

Compare that with finding yourself alone in the same location on a small boat at night with no shore in sight when a major storm unexpectedly rolls in. There is no greater reminder that we are part of nature then those moments we find ourselves powerless over it.

And then things grow even more ominous. With people living in the area for thousands of years, Europeans only arriving four hundred years ago, it turns out there is no shortage of supernatural accounts over the centuries, either.

Finding yourself alone in the middle of Lake Michigan can mean that sometimes it isn't just bad weather about which you should likely be concerned.

Personally, as a UFO investigator, after studying unusual phenomena in the Great Lakes area for over two decades, it has become clear that UFOs and other things that go bump in the night find themselves quite at home here.

While questionable events occur over land and water in Michigan with surprising regularity, including some that highly skeptical individuals try to argue can be explained away with prosaic explanations, the UFO wave of 1994, for example, goes well beyond what any reasonable mind could dismiss. Over the span of just a few short months, several hundred witnesses, including many individuals in law enforcement reported a wide variety of multi-colored UFOs doing fantastic maneuvers in the skies off the coast of Lake Michigan. The truth is a very strange event happened on a large scale.

On the night of March 8, 1994, during this sighting event, several impressively large flying saucers were seen along the western side of the state from the cities of Grand Haven down to Holland, before they suddenly dashed off over the Lake Michigan at speeds estimated at 3,000 miles per hour...but curiously never reached the shores of Indiana, Illinois, or Wisconsin.

Michigan boasts many hauntings, as well. Cryptid sightings, like Bigfoot are not uncommon, either. People also disappear, never to be seen again, and one has to wonder what is really at play in the deep waters and deep woods of this region.

Cheryl Carter has immersed herself in the mysteries of Lake Michigan, diving deep into local history to bring to the surface remarkable and eerie accounts to remind us that we don't know nearly everything about our natural surroundings and what supernatural things they hide.

Be prepared to learn some things that may just keep you clinging to shore, rather than gathering courage enough to ever venture into what some call, with good reason, the Lake Michigan Triangle.

Bill Konkolesky
State Director Michigan MUFON

Introduction

There are places on this earth that feel eerie, unnatural, sacred, mystical, or are revered so unique that they are thought to belong to the gods. According to some, the earth holds on to secrets; secrets that whisper of mystical energy, frequency, and vibrations. The ancients knew of the special powers of these anomalous places; places that hint to the possibility of stepping through a doorway enabling one to traverse time and move through dimensions.

Moreover, the Earth's surface is endowed with mysterious triangular patterns that possess secrets of their own. At first glance, these areas may appear peaceful and inviting radiating an addicting energy. And yet, they have a hunger, luring people to venture into their wilds, only to capture their souls forbidding them to ever leave these …

…DIMENSIONS

Chapter 1
Alaskan Triangle

Alaska is the northern most state in the United States. To the east are the Canadian Yukon Territory and the province of British Columbia, the Arctic Ocean on the north, and the Pacific Ocean to the west and south with Russian Siberia further across the Bering Strait. The eastern tip containing the Aleutian Islands has an island named Semisopochnoi, deriving its name from the Russian word meaning "having seven hills," that reaches across the 180th meridian which divides the Western and Eastern Hemisphere. Although being the largest and youngest of the volcanic islands in the Aleutians, it is actually the result of a collapsed volcano and the seven hills are volcanic peaks.

The name Alaska is derived from the Alent word "alyeska" meaning "great land."Alaska was once owned by Russia, but following the end of the Civil War, U.S. Secretary of State William Seward, thinking this land would help open a trade route with Asia, entered into negations with Russian Minister Eduard de Stoeki for the purchase of Alaska. On March 30, 1867, a treaty was signed and Congress ratified it despite the objection of President Andrew Johnson. This now added 586,412 square miles of new territory to the United States with the purchase of $7.2 million, a mere two cents per acre. It would be known as the Alaskan Territory until it became a state in 1959 making it the 49th state in the union. Some opponents considered the land useless and referred to it as "Steward's Folly" or "Steward's Icebox." That was until 1896, when gold was discovered there.

Alaska is known as "The Last Frontier" due to the fact that there are vast areas of land yet to be accurately charted, mapped, or even explored. In addition, there are few roads and many remote locations can only be accessed by plane or boat.

Part of Alaska, "The Land of the Midnight Sun," is located above the Arctic Circle. What this means is that from that point north, every year includes one day of 24-hour sunlight and one day of 24-hour darkness. There will be more days of 24-hour daylight and 24-hour darkness the further north you go. At the poles, there are six months between sunrise and sunset. This occurs at the equinoxes in late March and September. The area of Alaska that lies north of the 60th parallel stays light 24 hours for three months and dark for three months.

Human habitation began here around 10,000 B.C. It is believed that people migrated from Asia to North America across a land bridge known as the Beringia or Bering Strait. It is thought that when lower ocean levels, resulting from glaciers locking vast amounts of water, exposed a wide stretch of sea floor, people were able travel across. However, despite its vast land mass it is the third least populated of the states.

Alaska is a land of majestic beauty, however it is also a place where the tranquil earth sometimes decides to move in unpredictable ways causing tremendous earthquakes. One reason is because the Pacific plates and North American plates are constantly fighting for position atop the mantle. On March 27, 1964 at 5:36 P.M. the Great Alaskan or Good Friday Earthquake occurred when the Aleutian Megathrust, a fault between the Pacific plates and the North American plates ruptured near College Fjord near Price William Sound. In geological terms it is known as a subduction zone earthquake which is caused by an oceanic plate sinking under a continental plate. The earthquake measuring 9.2 and lasting four minutes and thirty-eight seconds was the most powerful recorded in North American history and the 2nd in recorded history. Rock slides, ground fissures, collapsing building, and tsunamis up to 200 feet high occurred when the ocean floor shifted killing 131 people.

The largest on-land earthquake in North America measuring 7.9 struck the Denali fault in 2002. Alaska accounts for seven out of the ten largest earthquakes in the United States, three of the eight largest earthquakes in the world, and claims 11% of the world's earthquakes. On average, there are 1,000 earthquakes each month varying in magnitude.

There are also instances when the unrelenting forces beneath the earth decide to demonstrate their mighty power by spewing molten magna into the air. Alaska is home to more than forty active volcanoes that have erupted at least once since 1760. In fact, 89% of the active volcanoes in the United States are in Alaska with most of them occurring along the Alaska Peninsula and Aleutian Islands. They are part of what is known as the "Ring of Fire" that surrounds much of the Pacific Ocean. The Ring of Fire is a 25,000 mile horseshoe shape consisting of 452 volcanoes, more than 75% of the world's active and dormant volcanoes. Here are 90% of the earth's earthquakes, 81% of the world's largest earthquakes, and all but three of the world's largest volcanic eruptions of the last 11,700 years.

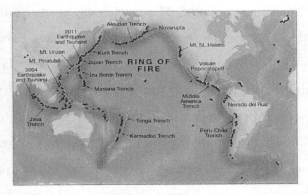

The Ring of Fire

On June 6, 1912, around 1:00 p.m. the skies darkened and the sun disappeared when about 400 miles southwest of Anchorage, the most powerful volcanic explosion of the 20th Century occurred as the Novarupta Volcano erupted and continued to erupt for three days. A Plinian style eruption similar to the eruption of Mount Vesuvius in 79 A.D. that destroyed the cities of Pompeii and Herculaneun, ejected columns of volcanic debris and hot gases high into the stratosphere about thirty miles above the earth. Magna produced was at a volume of 3.1 cubic miles which is thirty times more than the 1980 eruption of Mount St. Helens. Volcanic ash filled the valley covering an area of forty square miles which in some places was up to 700 feet deep. Following the eruption, thousands of fumaroles formed that vented steam from the ash. Fumarole is from the Latin word "fumes" meaning "smoke." This occurs when an opening in the earth's crust emits steam and gases the likes of which include carbon dioxide, hydrogen chloride, sulfur dioxide, and hydrogen sulfide. Steam forms when superheated water condenses and pressure causes it to emerge from the ground. When Robert F. Griggs, reporter for National Geographic Magazine, arrived to do an article what he witnessed prompted him to name the area "Valley of 10,000 Smokes."

Valley of 10,000 Smokes

The Alaskan Triangle is a vast area measuring 200,000 unforgiving square miles of largely unexplored wilderness, forests, mountains, and desolate barren tundra. The borders begin at the Barrow Mountain range in the far north, Anchorage in the south, extends to Juneau in the southeast, then back up to Barrow again.

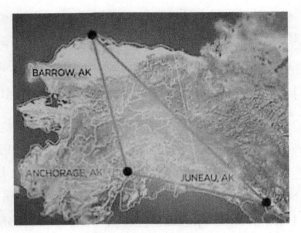

The Alaska Triangle

The Triangle is shrouded with secrets; secrets that it chooses not to share. The mysterious Alaskan wilderness with its untouched beauty whispers to unsuspecting visitors luring them into her wilds with the promise of adventure only to capture their souls and never allowing them to return. Since 1988, there have been 16,000 people who have vanished. That is more missing per capita than anywhere else on earth.

The Disappearance of the Cessna N1812H

One of the most highly profiled disappearances occurred on October 16, 1972. At 9:00 a.m., Democratic House Majority Leader Hale Boggs of Louisiana, Alaska House of Representative Nicholas Begich, an aide Russell

Brown, and their pilot Don Jonz boarded a twin-engine Cessna 310 Aircraft with the tail number N1812H for a flight from Anchorage to Juneau to attend an election rally for Begich. Jonz was a military veteran with more than 17,000 hours of flight experience. He filled out a flight plan indicating that he planned to fly southeast over the Turnagain Arm of Cook Inlet, through Portage Pass, over Prince William Sound to Juneau, and then on to Yakutat. From there he would fly directly to Juneau. The flight would take about 3 ½ hours and the plane carried six hours of fuel.

At 9:09, the pilot inquired about projected weather conditions. He was told the forecast was 1 ½ miles visibility with the fog, some icy rain, and turbulent head winds. That was the last known communication from the plane. When the plane had not reached its destination as schedule, the tower tried contacting them, but was unsuccessful.

Unfortunately, there were two pivotal factors that may have influenced their fate. The plane was not equipped with any anti-icing equipment and it was thought it might not have an emergency location transmitter which when activated transmits radio signals on the aviation common emergency frequencies. These signals can then be traced back to their source enhancing search and rescue efforts. The disappearance sparked a major search that lasted for thirty-

16

nine days covering over 325,000 miles. It included over 400 aircraft, dozens of boats, including twelve from the National Guard. No trace of the plane or the men was ever discovered. On December 29, 1972, when the search was terminated, they were declared dead.

Boggs Search Abandoned As Alaskan Winter Comes

ANCHORAGE, Alaska (AP) — After 39 futile days, the search for House Democratic Leader Hale Boggs has been abandoned because of the onset of winter.

Boggs, Alaska Rep. Nick Begich and two other men have been missing since Oct. 16 on a flight from Anchorage to Juneau.

Air Force Maj. Ken Shelley said the search, officially suspended Friday, will be reopened if any new clues or significant information is uncovered.

Aboard the plane were Boggs, 58; Begich, 40; Russell L. Brown, 37, an aide to Begich, and Don E. Jonz, 38, the pilot.

In Washington, Mrs. Boggs said she was deeply grateful for the effort "and especially for the heart" that had gone into the search.

Official proceedings are expected to begin in Alaska within a few days that could lead to declaring open the House seats to which Boggs and Begich were re-elected. Both wives of the missing congressmen said friends have encouraged them to run for the seats.

Daily Star - October 16, 1972

Hale Boggs

Nicholas Begich

Did weather conditions play a role in the disappearance? Yes, that was a possibility, however theorists think otherwise. Some believe the crash was deliberate or perhaps was covered up by J. Edgar Hoover, the head of the FBI. In April, 1971, Hale Boggs having served on the Warren Commission had accused the FBI of wiretapping congressional phones and called for J. Edgar Hoover's resignation. He claimed that he knew why the wiretapping had occurred, and when his lawyers were through with their investigation, he was going to reveal his information to the public. However, Attorney General John Mitchell denied Bogg's allegations about the FBI.

Project Moon Dust
JFK and Marilyn Monroe

In addition, he also wanted to reopen the case of the 1963 John F. Kennedy assassination. Had JFK actually been killed by our government because he was about to disclose what really happened at Roswell, New Mexico? Was it because he had directed the CIA to release highly classified files to NASA, the National Aeronautics and Space Administration? Or was it because he instructed James Edwin Webb administrator of NASA to develop by February 1,

1964, a program with the Soviet Union concerning joint space and lunar exploration?

Declassified documents reveal that JFK saw the alien UFO craft that crashed at Roswell, New Mexico. He saw other debris and alien bodies when he visited the Air Force base at Area 51 in Nevada.

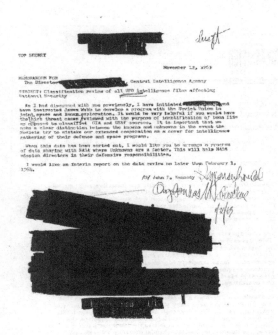

November 12, 1963 - Memo To: the CIA From: JFK
Data Sharing with NASA

```
FTD WRIGHT PATTERSON AFB

C O N F I D E N T I A L STATE 227792

E.O. 11652: GDS
TAGS:PINR, TSPA, UN, IV
SUBJECT: PROJECT MOONDUST

REFS:   A. USDAO 0427 (DTG 080948Z NOV 73)
        B. STATE 221655   C. STATE A-6343,
```

Project Moon Dust
Wright Patterson Air Force Base Dayton, OH

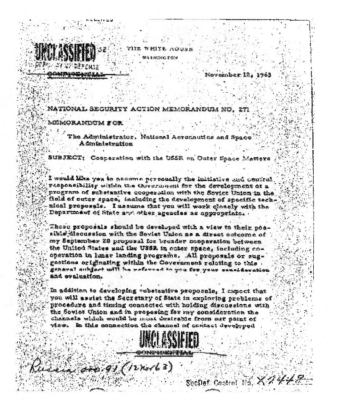

November 18, 1963 Memo To: NASA From : JFK
Program with the USSR on Space and Lunar Exploration

An unclassified CIA Wiretap document dated August 3, 1962, and signed by James Angleton of the CIA provided information obtained from Marilyn Monroe's phone conversations with Attorney General Robert Kennedy and journalist Dorothy Kilgallen of the New York Journal American. Marilyn made numerous calls to Robert complaining about the manner in which she was being treated by him and JFK after they had ended their intimate relationships with her. She made calls to Dorothy Kilgallen wherein she threatened to hold a press conference releasing such conversations that she and JFK had involving Roswell that she recorded in her "diary of secrets."

Also referenced in the document was Project Moon Dust which was the code name for a covert operation that recovered debris from space craft that had survived reentry from space to earth. Thirty-six hours later she was discovered dead of an apparent drug overdose.

After the Kennedy Assassination, Dorothy Kilgallen, a journalist intrigued with organized crime continued probing into what she called a conspiracy. She held copious secret interviews and phone calls with those involved such as Jack Ruby. In her last article she stated, "The story is not going to die as long as there's a real reporter alive."

The following day on November 8, 1965, she was discovered dead in her Manhattan, New York townhouse. Coincidentally, cause of death was determined a suicide.

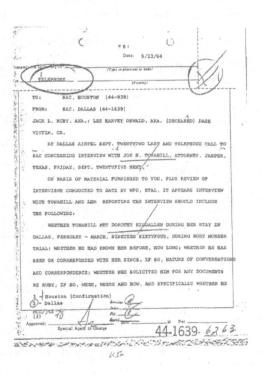

September 23, 1964 - FBI Memo #44-1639-6263
Connecting Kilgallen to Jack Ruby
To: SAC –Special Agent in Charge FBI Houston, TX

Dorothy Killagallen   Marilyn Monroe

August 4, 1962 – Marilyn Monroe Death Certificate
Probable Suicide

Mob Related Theory

Another theory concludes that Nicholas Begich was the target instead of Boggs. Less than seventeen months after his disappearance, Peggy Begich his widow married Jerry Max Pasley whom she had been secretly seeing for some time. Pasley, a hit man connected with the Mafia worked with Joseph Bonanno and Peter Licavoli. Bonnanno was the head of one of the most powerful crime families in the country for over thirty years.

In 1994, Pasley was convicted of killing a man in a Tucson hotel. Realizing he was going to spend the remainder of his life in prison, during his trial he told the judge that he wanted to come clean about the other terrible murders he had committed. He provided authorities details to several unsolved murders. Little did they know he would also confess to the murder of Nicholas Begich.

He stated that while he and Peggy were secretly seeing each other, she gave him many lavish gifts, one of which gave him co-ownership in a bar. One of the partners was the man he had given the suitcase to in 1972. One day while the two of them were having drinks, the man became drunk and told him that the briefcase had contained a high-tech bomb which he placed on Pan Alaska N1812H right before it left on its final flight that day.

In 1972, he was handed a briefcase by one of Bonanno's men in Arizona. His instructions were to take it to Anchorage where he was to turn it over to two men. After the exchange took place, he flew back to Arizona, but not before he was told "something big" was about to happen. It was soon afterward that the plane disappeared.

Jerry Max Pasley   Joseph Bonanno   Peter Licavoli

Anchorage Police Sergeant Mike Grims went to Arizona to interview Pasley in prison. Upon returning to Anchorage, he immediately contacted the local FBI. When he hadn't heard back from the agent, he called her again. However, fearing their conversation would be overheard, she insisted that they meet somewhere outside of her office. Once away from the office, she further stated that when her boss called the FBI headquarters in Washington D. C. with the information, he was ordered, "You will do nothing there. You will send everything you have to us." Then without interviewing Pasley the FBI immediately shut down the investigation.

Let it also be noted that two days after the plane's disappearance the United States Coast Guard station in Long Beach, California received a phone call from an anonymous caller claiming that he knew the plane had crashed. They forwarded the phone number to the FBI who presumably interviewed him, but nothing became of it.

Also at that time, a ham radio operator reported that he received a distress call. The FBI verified the coordinates, but never notified the search party. Twenty years later, a mysterious box was sent to a pilot friend of Don Joze. Inside the box, were FBI classified files covering the two government officials and an account of a cover-up concerning the missing plane.

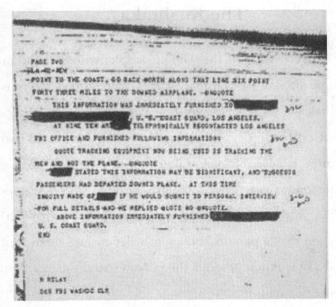

Ham Radio Call forwarded to the FBI

There are a plethora of reasons for the inexplicable disappearances in the Alaska Triangle. The area comprises dense forests, massive glaciers, hidden caves, and deep crevasses in which a downed aircraft or even the most experienced hiker could very easily be lost, hidden, and possibly buried beneath snow. In addition, there are dangerous wild animals that one might encounter as well as malevolent entities.

The Kushtaka

According to the Tlingit people, whose name means "People of the Tides," there exists a creature known as the Kushtaka, a huge shape-shifting entity that is half man and half otter that lives deep within the woods. It is said that the creature is capable of taking your darkest fears and manifesting them into a hellish reality. The Kushtaka is credited with shape-shifting into a human form of perhaps someone that a person knows in order to lure them into the woods. Once there it steals the person's soul preventing them from reincarnation.

Kushtaka

UFOs and JAL Flight 1628

Some believe the disappearances are other-worldly related as the Triangle is a hot spot for extraterrestrial activity. On November 17, 1986, a Japanese Boeing 174-200F cargo aircraft Flight 1628 was flying over Anchorage on its return from Paris. The crew included Captain Kenju Terauchi, an ex-fighter pilot and senior pilot with more than 10,000 hours flight experience, co-pilot 1st Officer Takanori Tamefuji, and flight engineer Yoshio Tsukuba.

At 17:11, they encountered two objects to their left that continued to follow them for about 400 miles as they passed through the Alaskan Triangle. One of the objects appeared to be twice the size of the aircraft while the other was smaller. The crew reported seeing flashing lights following their plane. Air traffic controllers also tracked something unidentifiable on their radar that was as close as five miles away from the plane. The pilot said that at one point one of the aircrafts appeared directly in front of the plane at a very close distance.

Captain Terauchi described the crafts as disappearing within the clouds and reappearing as if it did not want to be observed. He said, "The thing was flying as if there was no such thing as gravity. It sped up quickly, stopped, then flew at our speed, in our direction, so that it appeared to be standing still. The next instance, it changed course like it had overcome gravity which is impossible for a normal plane to do

17:19, control was notified. At this point, the UFOs were being tracked on military and civilian radar, and verified by a high level administrator of the Federal Aviation Administration (FAA). In an attempt to elude the UFOs, the pilot requested permission from the ground crew to fly at a lower altitude. However, even after making several attempts, he could not elude them. The encounter continued to last about thirty-two minutes, before the UFOs just suddenly disappeared.

Where the objects disappeared, Captain Terauchi noticed a pale band of light that mirrored their altitude, speed, and direction. He informed Anchorage Air Traffic Control, however they saw nothing on their radar. Upon flying over Fairbanks, the city lights helped illuminate the object, to which he believed to be the outline of a giant spacecraft which he referred to as the "Mother Ship."

JAL Flight 1628

Pilot Says UFO Dwarfed His 747 Jet

Anchorage, Alaska

A veteran pilot whose UFO sighting was confirmed on radar screens said the thing was so enormous that his Japan Air Lines cargo jet—a Boeing 747—was tiny compared with the mysterious object.

Captain Kenju Terauchi also said there were two other unidentified objects — smaller than his cargo carrier — that did not appear on radar.

Terauchi, his co-pilot and flight engineer all told Federal Aviation Administration investigators that they saw UFO lights as they flew over Alaska on a Europe-to-Japan flight.

"They were flying parallel and then suddenly approached very close," said Terauchi, 47, who received FAA permission to take whatever evasive action was necessary to avoid the UFO. The object appeared for a time on FAA and Air Force radar and on the radar screen in the cockpit of JAL flight 1628.

Terauchi spoke to United Press International on Tuesday, describing the UFO incident of November 17 that was revealed by the FAA on Monday. Additional FAA data released Tuesday again confirmed that government radar picked up the object.

Terauchi, a pilot for 29 years, said he briefly glimpsed the large unknown object in silhouette, and he said, "It was a very big one — two times bigger than an aircraft carrier."

Terauchi made a drawing of the large UFO, showing it as a giant walnut-shaped object with big bulges above and below a wide flattened brim.

United Press International

Anchorage Daily News – November 18, 1986

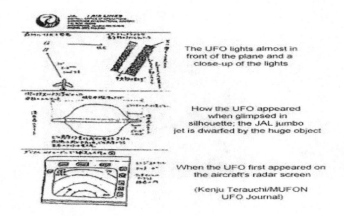

The UFO lights almost in front of the plane and a close-up of the lights

How the UFO appeared when glimpsed in silhouette; the JAL jumbo jet is dwarfed by the huge object

When the UFO first appeared on the aircraft's radar screen

(Kenju Terauchi/MUFON UFO Journal)

MUFON Journal - Drawings by Captain Terauchi
Aircraft Radar Screen and Spacecraft

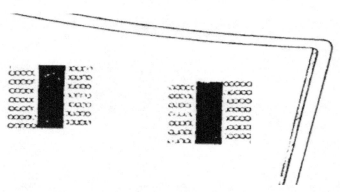

Spacecraft as seen through the cockpit window

Captain Kenju Terauchi

```
FEDERAL AVIATION ADMINISTRATION
ALASKAN REGION
701 C Street, Anchorage, Alaska, 99513


DECEMBER 30, 1986
CONTACT: PAUL STEUCKE, FAA, PUBLIC AFFAIRS, ALASKA
         (907) 271-5296

The following information constructed from personal handwritten
notes, has been provided to Paul Steucke, FAA Public Affairs
Officer, Alaskan Region, by Jim Derry, Manager, FAA Security
Division, Alaskan Region, and constitutes the information
obtained in personal interviews held the evening of Novmber 17,
1986, at Anchorage International Airport, with the flight crew of
Japan Air Lines flight 1628, enroute from Europe and Iceland/ to
Toyko, via Anchorage, Alaska.

Attending the interview were: Jim Derry, Manager, Security
Division, FAA: Ron Mickle, Investigator, FAA Security: Jack
Wright, Investigator, FAA Flight Standards District Office, the
Manager of the JAL Anchorage Office: and the flight crew -
Captain Kenjyu Terauchi; First Officer Takonori Tamefuji; and
Flight Engineer Yoshio Tsukuda.

The interviews were in response to the sighting of unknown and
unidentified air traffic which accompanied the flight from the
Alaska Canadian border on the north along a flight plan which
flows approximately from Ft. Yukon, Alaska, to Fairbanks, to
Anchorage.


NOTES:

*  FLIGHT NUMBER JAL 1628, Dep. Reykjavik, Iceland.
*  ADIZ, HL529...J529... (Airway numbers) Contact at POTAT()
*  Visual contact..can see FAI, over FAI did 360 degrees.
*  S. MJ-125, Route


continued...
```

December 30, 1986 – JAL Flight 1628
Federal Aviation Administration – Alaskan Region

Page two, JAL #1628, Notes, FAA, Alaska

* Used onboard color radar, located aircraft, 7 miles.
* Size: "As big as B747 or larger, erratic movement."
* Lights: Yellow, Amber, Green, No red. Rotating Beacon. Many
  small lights.
* One object, two sets of lights.
* Speed of JAL B747: .84 Mach, (Approximately 525 knots)
* ATC (Air Traffic Control) picked up target.
* Target broke off ---40 N of TKA (Talkeetna)
* Radio: Received static only in VHF mode. (Abnormal)
* JAL aircraft on instrument navigation.
* Flight Crew observation: Normal, professional, rational, no
  drug or alcohol involvement.
* Drawings of situation provided by Captain.
* Normal language difficulty between flight crew and
  interviewer.

** Note: Exact conversion to mph or knts is difficult as it
        varies due to evelation (air density), weather, wind,
        etc.)

END.

Captain Terauchi's Statement

At the Federal Aviation Administration (FAA), Vice Admiral Donald D. Enger was briefed concerning the incident. The following day, he and John Callahan, the Division Chief of the Accidents and Investigations branch held a briefing where the video was shown. Included at the meeting were members of the FBI, CIA, President Ronald

Reagan's Scientific Study Team, and Captain Terauchi. Upon the conclusion of the meeting, everyone present was informed that this incident was a secret and that the meeting never took place. Upon concluding the meeting, officials took possession of the presented data. John Callahan managed to retain the FAA's original report, Captain Terauchi's report, and the original video.

On March 5, 1987, after a three month investigation, the FAA was prepared to release their findings at a press conference.

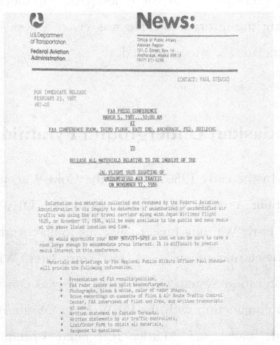

Press Conference Announcement #87-08

However, although officials at the FAA considered the data to represent the first instance of recorded radar data indicating a UFO, instead of disclosure, Paul Steucke, the FAA Public Information Officer in Anchorage, issued a retraction. He stated that what the controllers actually observed was a "split radar image." There was not enough information to confirm that something was actually there and the flight crew was merely seeing lights.

In December 1986, Captain Terauchi gave an interview to two journalists from Kyodo News in Japan. Shortly afterward, Japan Air Lines (JAL) grounded him for disclosing the information. He was given a desk job, but a few years later, he was reinstated.

Alaskan Underground Pyramid

In the early 1950's during the Cold War, the United States built a radar system known as the DEW Line or Distant Early Warning Line, to give the military early warning of a Soviet nuclear strike. A few years later, White Alice Communication System known as WACS was constructed to work in conjunction with the DEW Line. "White Alice" was the code name for ALaska Integrated Communications

Enterprise a United States Air Force telecommunication network with eighty radio stations. It used a tropospheric scatter microwave radio signal for over-the-horizon links. Tropospheric scatter is a fairly secure method of transmitting radio waves making it extremely difficult to intercept the signals particularly if transmitted over open water. It uses radio waves at UHF and SHF frequencies that are randomly scattered as they pass through the upper layers of the troposphere, the lowest region of the atmosphere from the earth's surface. White Alice consisted of large parabolic, tropospheric scatter antennas and smaller microwave dishes for point to point links.

DEW – Distance Early Warning Line

WACS – ALaska Integrated Communications Enterprise
Code Name "White Alice"

On May 22, 1992, China conducted an underground nuclear test in Lon Por. Soon afterward, scientists in the United States began collecting a huge amount of seismic data in Alaska to assure that the underground test had not done any harm. What they detected was extremely high EMI or electromagnetic interference, but could not locate its exact origin. This data raised great concern considering this was such a remote location in the Alaskan wilderness. Was it somehow possible for a team of Soviet military engineers to be there undetected and perhaps secretly hidden underground with some sort of EMI generator that   could disrupt White Alice and the DEW Line Communications?

This prompted scientists in Alaska to perform a seismic recording study which measured the reverberations through the earth's mantle. What they found through this test was astounding for it led to the discovery of an underground structure, but it was not what they expected. Further tests indicated that it appeared to be an underground pyramid.

The Army began an extensive underground project code name Dark Pyramid. The pyramid located at 63°17'51.40 N and 152°31'24.489 W, lies 150 feet beneath the earth's surface. Its points include Juneau in the southeast, the Barrow mountain range in the north, and Anchorage in the west. It stands 1150 feet tall with each side measuring

1510 feet which is twice the size of the Great Pyramid of Giza in Egypt that measures 755 feet.

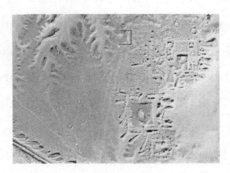

Aerial View of Underground Pyramid

In 1992, Channel 13 Anchorage was the first to air the story reporting that scientists were conducting seismic recording experiments and believed they had discovered the dimensions of a pyramid structure about fifty miles from Mt. McKinley. U.S. Counter-intelligence Warrant Officer Doug Mutschler, stationed at Fort Richardson was watching television with thirty other military members when the breaking news story came over Channel 13. The next day, he went to the news station to get a detailed copy of the report. The station denied ever reporting that story and that the story never existed. As he was leaving the station, he was approached by a film editor who told him that the station did indeed broadcast the story, but he could not give him any information.

Years later he tried to search through government files in hopes of finding more information. He was approached by two officials who informed him that he had no authorization to be looking at such files and told him to leave. In 2012, he contacted Linda Moulton Howe, a journalist and UFO Researcher, with his story. On July 26, 2012, she broadcasted a recorded interview on Coast-to-Coast a.m. radio where Mutschler related to her the story about a heavily guarded pyramid built with alien technology that actually generates its own energy. The structure was built in such a manner that the magnetic declination was pointed to the North Pole. How this structure came to be and who actually was involved in its creation remains a mystery. Was it man-made or were there alien connotations? Conspiracy theorists believe the government knows.

Another theory for disappearances is that the Alaska Triangle comprises one of the vile vortices. A vortex is a point where two ley lines intersect. The source of the lines begins in the Peruvian Mountains where two ley lines, the Rainbow Serpent Line and the Plumbed Serpent Line, intersect at Lake Titicaca. One of these lines, the Plumbed Serpent Line which is the largest on earth, runs under the

Gulf of Alaska, an arm of the North Pacific Ocean, and along the fault lines. Its coordinates are 61° 58'N and 149° 24'W.

A vortex created by gravitational pull can cause distortion such as extreme electric, magnetic, and electromagnetic anomalies. This can have different effects on people such as hallucinations and visions, confusion, and disorientation. Instruments such as a compass will malfunction. It is also believed that a vortex may be a passageway into another realm.

Alaska is a land of enchantment shrouded in mysteries; mysteries that we may never be privy to. Perhaps the only few that have knowledge of her mysteries are the ones who never returned to tell their stories.

Chapter 2
Bennington Triangle

Located between the Taconic and Green Mountains, Bennington, Vermont is a popular place for outdoor enthusiasts. The Green Mountains run south to north and extend 250 miles up to the border of Quebec, Canada. Prior to the arrival of the colonists, the land belonged to the Western Abenaki people whose name means "People of the Dawn."

Bennington is one of the first charted towns of Colonial America. It is where in 1770, Ethan Allen, his brother Ira, and cousin Seth Warner formed the Green Mountain Boys a militia whose objective was to defend the property rights of local landowners. The Green Mountain Boys were rebels who were sometimes known to resort to unconventional methods in order to assure justice.

Eventually, they became part of the Continental Army. On May 10, 1775, they were instrumental in helping the American Colonies during the Revolutionary War by seizing the British Fort Ticonderoga and returning stolen

artillery, especially canons, back to Boston Harbor positioning them on higher points severely limiting the options of the British. Ticonderoga meaning "between two waters" was a key point of access to both Canada and the Hudson River Valley. Gaining control of the fort afforded the colonies reassurance that they would not be attacked through Canada and impeded the British's communication. During the Battle of Bennington on August 16, 1977, they prevented the British from their attempt at seizing the munitions stored in Bennington which would be used during the Battle of Saratoga a turning point of the Revolution.

Arsenic Murders

It is the birthplace of Elizabeth Woodley Van Volkenburgh known for the "arsenic murders." Elizabeth first married at the age of twenty and together they had four children. However, six years later, her husband mysteriously died. Years later, she finally admitted she had poisoned him by slipping arsenic into his rum. Her second marriage was to John Van Volkenburgh, but just a few years into their life together, he too mysteriously died. This time she had slipped arsenic into his brandy.

His family immediately became suspicious and notified the police. Elizabeth quickly ran away attempting to elude them by hiding in a neighbor's barn. However, her plan failed when she fell from the hayloft breaking her leg in the process. She was immediately arrested and charged with John's murder. Before handing down her sentence, the judge anticipated her showing remorse for what she had done. Unfortunately, looking back at that day and remembering how she watched as her husband died a horrible death, she said, "If the deed could have been recalled, I would have done it with all my heart." Upon hearing this, the judge sentenced her to death by hanging.

When the day came for her hanging on January 24, 1846, it was not done in the usual manner. Instead because of her broken leg, she was carried to the gallows in her rocking chair where she sat contently rocking as the trap door was opened.

In the graveyard next to the old First Church is the final resting place of the poet Robert Lee Frost whose epitaph reads, "I had a lover's quarrel with the world." Although he never lived in Bennington, he did spend every summer there and was inspired to write these words about the forest:

> "The woods are lonely, dark and deep.
> But I have promises to keep
> And miles to go before I sleep."

How apropos that Frost so eloquently described a place that some might consider quite mysterious. This is because Bennington is also known as the center of the Bennington Triangle. The triangle spans a large stretch of wilderness in Southwest Vermont within the Glastenbury Mountain area comprising the towns of Bennington, Woodford, Shaftsbury, Somerset and Glastenbury which was once a logging community and now a ghost town.

Bennington Triangle

The Long Trail

Within this triangle is the Long Trail, a hiking trail in Vermont that is the oldest long distance trail in the United States 272 miles in length and running from the Massachusetts state line near Williamstown, north through Vermont and to the Canadian border.

It was through the vision of James P. Taylor, the Assistant Headmaster of the Vermont Academy, that construction began in 1910. It is known as Vermont's "Footpath in the Wilderness" reaching along the main ridge of the Green Mountain range, coinciding with the Appalachian Trail for almost one hundred miles in the southern part of the state. It traverses all the Green Mountain's major summits including Stratton Mountain, Killington Peak, Mount Abraham, Mount Ellen, Camel's Hump, Mount Mansfield and Jay Peak all of which reach heights over 3,000 feet and Glastenbury Mountain which is 3,747 feet. The trail can best be described as back country with forests, swift running streams, ponds, rugged climbing peaks and bogs.

The Long Trail

Bennington Monster

This area has always had claims of many mysterious phenomena: strange sounds, anomalous lights, feelings of disorientation, people going insane, cryptids and UFO sightings. The Algonquin people who inhabited the land from as far back as 8500 B.C. chose to avoid the land west of Glastenbury Mountain believing it to be a powerful place where there was convergence of the four winds. Believing it to be a passageway to another world, they used it as a burial ground.

European settlers told tales of bizarre creatures and mysterious lights over Glastenbury Mountain. The first sighting was in the early 19th century, as a stagecoach was making its way over the mountain near Glastenbury near what is now Route 9 in Woodford. As darkness began to fall, they found themselves caught in the middle of a torrential downpour. With visibility being so poor and the realization that the rain would surely wash out the road, the driver was forced to stop in the mountain wilderness. He jumped down from his seat and with lantern in hand, he tried to better assess the surroundings. It was then that he noticed something peculiar being illuminated by the lantern light. As he walked closer, just up ahead he could make out very large footprints in the mud.

Surely these had to be fresh since the rain had not yet washed them away. Upon closer examination, they appeared to be widely spaced suggesting that whatever had made them was of tremendous stature. Behind him, he heard the horses begin to whine as if they sensed danger. He called back to the passengers asking them to come over and inspect the footprints. Just as a few of them began to step out, the horses started going wild when something struck the side of the stagecoach with great force. Everyone hurried to get out just in time before the entire stagecoach tumbled over on its side. As they stood there in the pouring rain, out of the darkness emerged a tall hairy creature about eight feet tall with two glowing eyes. It stared at them for a few moments and then ran off into the woods. They called him The Bennington Monster and he would be seen many times after that.

Bennington Monster

Without A Trace

In 1999, "The Blair Witch Project" told the story of three student filmmakers hiking into the Black Hills of Burkittsville, Maryland to film a documentary about a local legend known as the Blair Witch. They soon found themselves lost in the woods, encountering strange lights and sounds, going insane, and disappearing. Although this movie was fiction, the Glastenbury Mountain's story is real.

The Blair Witch Project

The mystery began to unfold in 1945 when people started to disappear without a trace and it would continue for five years. November 12, 1945, seventy-four year old Middie Rivers an experienced hunting and fishing guide lead a group of four hunters into the woodlands near the mountain. As they began to head back down the Long Trail near Route 9 to their camp, Rivers somehow got separated from the group around Bickford Hollow. When he hadn't returned to camp, the men notified the authorities. Searchers were unable to locate him. The only clue was a single rifle shell near the stream that may or may not have been his. It appeared that the forest had swallowed him up.

74 - YEA
HUNTER L
FOR TWO DAYS

Local Searching Parties,
Summoned by Fire Siren
at. 5 a. m., Comb Woods
of Bickford Hollow

Middie Rivers, veteran hunter and fisherman who will be 75 years old next month is lost in Bickford Hollow, just "off the Long Trail" and up to noon time today the lost hunter had not been located. The last time he was seen so far as is known by relatives here was by Hollis Armstrong of Safford street, who met the hunter in the Hollow about 4 o'clock Monday afternoon. ... went to with a hunting party to quenna ces. Hunter's Rest with his son-in-law, Joe Learon, Jr. Friday night. He knows the woods and trails in that ...

The Bennington Banner
November 14, 1945

A year later, on December 1, 1946, Paula Jean Weldon an eighteen year old sophomore at Bennington College asked her roommate Elizabeth Parker if she wanted to go out for a hike. Elizabeth declined the offer so Paula hitchhiked alone to the trailhead between Bennington and Woodford Hollow and started north along the Long Trail. She was witnessed by many other hikers including a man by the name of Ernest Whitman who remembered asking her how far the trail went. She was also seen by a couple who were about a hundred yards behind her. They said they saw her take the trail around a rocky outcropping, but when they reached that spot, she was nowhere to be seen. When she failed to return to her dorm room and missed classes the next day, she was declared missing. Even though that trail was well-traveled and not secluded, a manhunt lead by the FBI never found a trace of her or her red jacket.

Paula Jean Weldon

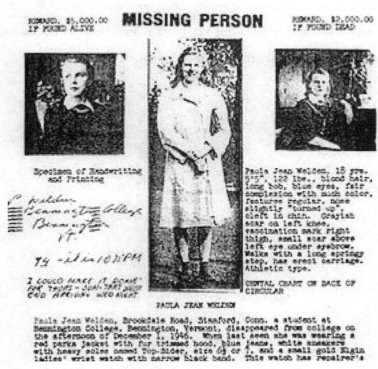

Paula Jean Weldon - Reward Flyer

Exactly three years to the day, on December 1, 1949, James E. Tetford, a war veteran was on his way back from a trip to Vermont where he had been visiting his parents. He boarded a bus at St. Alban's bound for Bennington along with fourteen other passengers, but never reached his destination. Some passengers aboard the bus reported that they saw him sleeping in his seat at the next to the last stop one moment and the next moment he was gone leaving all his luggage and wallet behind. Everyone was baffled as the bus had been in motion the entire time so there was no way he could have gotten off, but yet he was nowhere to be found when the bus finally reached its destination.

James E. Tetford

On October 12, 1950, while Mrs. Jepson was tending to the animals on the farm, her eight year old son Paul was playing near their truck. When she returned less than an hour later, the boy was nowhere to be found. The authorities searched the area with bloodhounds thinking they would easily find the young boy who was wearing a red jacket. The dogs tracked the boy to an area west of Glastenbury Mountain to the intersection of Chapel and East Roads and then lost the scent. This was the exact spot where Paula Weldon had gone missing. It wasn't until later that the boy's father made a most bizarre statement. He stated that his son was exhibiting an alarming desire to go up into the nearby mountains. It was almost as if they were beckoning him closer and luring him into their clutches.

Bennington Evening Banner
October 13, 1950

BENNINGTON EVENING BANNER
FRIDAY - OCTOBER 13, 1950

Rain-Soaked Posse Hunts White Chapel Woods For 8 Year Old Paul Jepson; Missing Since Late Thursday Afternoon; Bloodhound Search Fails

Bennington Evening Banner
October 13, 1950

Sixteen days later, on October 28, 1950, Freida Langer 53 and her cousin Herbert Elsner were camping with some friends near the Somerset Reservoir. Being familiar with the area, the two of them decide to go hiking. During the hike, Langer slipped and fell into a stream. Assuring her cousin that she was not injured, but being totally soaked, she proceeded to head back to the campsite to change her clothes. Since the campsite was nearby, she told him to wait there and she would be back shortly.

Elsner waited and became concerned when over an hour had passed and she had not returned. He made his way back to camp to see what was going on, but soon discovered that she was nowhere to be found and the others had not seen her. Together they searched the area with no luck and decided to contact the authorities. Even after five extensive searches using both dogs and helicopters, she could not be found. Then the following year on May 12, 1951, Langer's decomposed body was discovered in full view in an open clearing near Somerset Reservoir which was an area that had been extensively searched the prior year. The body was too decomposed to determine the cause of death.

Freda Langer

VERMONT AROUSED ABOUT PEOPLE LOST IN WOODS

Police, Worried Over Mysteries, Order Showdown Search For Mrs. Langer

Bennington Banner

So what actually happened to these people and why did all the disappearances abruptly stop after five years? Natives spoke of a mysterious enchanted rock which is said to swallow anything that steps upon it. Although nobody in modern times has seen this dangerous anomaly, or at least no one who has lived to tell about it, it is thought to be quite large enough for someone to actually stand upon it.

There is also the claim that the area contains gateways that are actually passageways to other dimensions and worlds. A person could step through these whether they intended to do so or not. Some researchers suggest that these gateways are opened periodically due to tectonic plate activity by means of plates found in this area. The Green Mountains are actually the result of a series of tectonic events producing a mixture of rock formations occurring hundreds of millions of years ago.

Tectonic Plate is the scientific theory describing the motion of seven large plates and movements of a larger number of small plates of the Earth's lithosphere since this process began about 3.5 billion years ago. The lithosphere is the rigid outer layer of the planet and is sixty miles thick. Churning currents in the molten rocks below create activity where the plates meet or divide. The movement of the plates creates three types of tectonic outcome: convergent, where plates move into one another; divergent, where plates move apart; and transform, where plates move sideways in relation to one another. They move at a rate of one-two inches per year.

Alien Abduction

Others attribute the disappearances to alien abduction. And it's rightfully so because there have been many reports of extraterrestrial and strange lights that have been spotted in the sky over Glastenbury for the past century. Whatever the case, it appears the mountain intends to never share its secrets with anyone. That is unless a person promises to never leave.

The first documented sighting of an unidentified flying object in America occurred within the triangle. On March 1, 1639, John Winthrop, the governor and cofounder of the Massachusetts Bay Colony, recorded in his journal what he said was a secondhand account of a witness, he described as a sober, discreet man, observing an unidentified flying object in the sky over the Muddy River in Boston. According to the story, James Everell and some others were rowing a boat one evening when they observed a strange bright green light in the sky. They watched as it stayed stationary and then began to glow brighter. It was approximately three yards square. It moved quickly and then changed direction and moved up and down. They continued to watch for about three hours until it moved "as swift as an arrow" towards Charlton. It was then that they realized their boat had gone one mile upstream. Nobody had a recollection of how they had gotten there.

Governor John Winthrop

Site of the first documented UFO sighting in America
March 1, 1639

On July 22, 1808, Cynthia Everett, a school teacher, recorded a very similar account in her diary. At around 10:00 p.m. she observed a rather strange light in the sky that appeared to come from the east. At first she thought it was a meteor, but because of its movement she wasn't sure what it was. As she watched, it darted across the sky, and then began to ascend and change direction descending yet not falling to the ground.

The Bluff Ledge Camp Abduction

According to MUFON, extraterrestrial events have continued throughout the years with more than 2800 sightings since 1940. One of the most famous was the Buff Ledge Camp Abduction.

On August 7, 1968, the swim team from Buff Ledge Girl's Camp took a trip to Burlington in order to compete in a meet. Michael Lap the 16 year old maintenance man and Janet Cornell the 19 year old water ski instructor were relaxing and enjoying some quiet time on the dock of Lake Champlain while enjoying the beautiful sunset. A bright light appeared in the southwest sky which they thought perhaps might be Venus. However, the light appeared to have movement and began moving downward. Three smaller lights emerged from the large light which had now rapidly ascended again before completely disappearing.

They watched as the three lights began to move over the lake performing strange maneuvers, upward spirals, and stop and go activity. Then as the lights began to move toward them, they formed a triangle, and emitted a vibrating sound similar to a thousand tuning forks.

The light on the right abruptly took off in a northerly direction while the one on the left departed to the south vanishing behind the trees.

The third light plunged into the lake causing a steady gale and three foot white-cap waves to spring up all over the lake. Dogs along the lake were heard howling, trees on the bluff began creaking, and branches were breaking from the force of the wind.

Three minutes later the light emerged from the lake and headed in their direction. Now Michael realized it was not a light, but actually a silver disc craft about 50 feet across that was incandescent as if glowing by its own light. Its edge contained a band of pulsating spectrum colored lights that flashed from left to right changing from purple to blue and green to red. It hovered about 20 feet above the water as if it were waiting; waiting to calculate its next move.

He glanced over at Janet hoping she could validate all this and it wasn't merely a dream. Unfortunately, he quickly came to the conclusion that she appeared to be in some sort of trance and unable to speak. The craft shot a beam of light at them giving them the sensation of floating. Their next thoughts would be hearing the swim team returning and watching the object in the sky again; the sky which was now totally dark.

Neither Michael nor Janet ever spoke of that night. After all, there was nothing much to remember except the strange lights in the sky. They went on to lead normal lives despite during the following years, experiencing strange dreams and anxiety. Finally, five years later, Michael decided it would be best to contact CUFOS, the Center for UFO Studies.

Walter N. Webb, one of the leading investigators of all time and a UFO witness himself, was assigned the case. He was very interested in this particular case having been the initial investigator of the Barney and Betty Hill event seven years earlier. After listening to Michael's account of the evening, he suggested they attempt regressive hypnosis. This treatment would be used to unlock suppressed memories and would enable them to recall the details of the missing time.

Hoping to obtain answers and relief for their anxiety, they readily agreed. While under hypnosis, they both recalled similar events. Michael recalled the beam of light feeling like a warm liquid and lifting him up into the craft. Janet was already there on a silver table being examined. She said she felt cold and something was pinching her and taking samples of skin, hair, and blood. Michael remembered the beings as about 5 feet tall, greenish-blue, big eyes, and three pointed web-like fingers. They had no mouth and communicated telepathically. When he asked one being why they were there, he was told, "our mission is to make life like ours in other places," and "we are concerned about your atomic testing."

Walter N. Webb also interviewed others who were at the Camp during that time. Although they did not witness the incident, they concurred seeing strange lights in the sky around the same time as Michael and Janet. He submitted his report to J. Allen Hynek who included it in his book "Encounter at Buff Ledge: A UFO Case History."

© Michael Lap drawings
Regressive Hypnosis

Large eyes and web-like hands

The beings related to him telepatically that their mission was to "make life like ours ... other places."

Chapter 3
Big Lick Triangle

There is an area that was once glaciated land that is located on the crest of the Cincinnati Arch. The Cincinnati Arch, approximately 2269 miles long, extends from north of Dayton, Ohio southward to just beyond Lexington, Kentucky and is bisected by the Ohio River. It was formed during the Paleozoic Era, which began about 541 million years ago and lasted to 251 million years ago. It was the greatest extinction event in Earth's history.

During that time, the land elevations were much lower than today and the sea levels were much higher. Sea levels continued to rise and the climate was very hot due to the high concentration of CO_2 in the atmosphere giving it a greenhouse effect. Large volcanoes had major eruptions which are evident in the beds of volcanic ash that has been preserved. Geologists estimate that the eruptions may have generated over 5000 times the volume of volcanic ash as was produced by Mt. St. Helen in 1980.

Scientists believe that during the last Ice Age, the late Pleistocene Epoch, 2,588,000 - 11,700 years ago, there had been an asteroid or comet collision with the atmosphere resulting in an Ice Age; one of the coldest times in the last 600 million years, causing the largest mass extinction in Earth's history. It took life on land 30 million years to recover.

In 2007, despite there not being any evidence of a massive crater in which such an impact may have occurred, there has been discovered microscopic melted rock formations high in platinum, spherules, and nanodiamonds in ancient soil layers all over the world. These particles rich in iron formed at an extreme temperature of 3,600 F cannot naturally form on Earth. Therefore, it is evident that these particles could have only been the result of a comet or asteroid impact. It is estimated these fragments are the remnants of a very large comet measuring 4 kilometers or 12,123 feet.

In theory, a comet would have been capable of producing enormous fires resulting in the melting of the North American ice sheet. This would in turn, send cold water into the oceans disrupting the circulation of ocean currents which normally are responsible for global heat transport. In 1694, Edmund Halley suggested that a world-wide flood, such as recorded in biblical times, most likely occurred as the result of a comet. This hypothesis known as the Clovis Comet derives its name from the Clovis culture that inhabited North America at that time and suddenly vanished.

This area is also known as the Big Lick Triangle. The boundaries start at Pope Lick in Louisville, Kentucky, north 58 miles to French Lick in Indiana, then 116 miles across to Big Bone Lick in Kentucky, and 83 miles back to Louisville. The region is bordered by the Wabash River to the east, the Ohio to the south, and the Mississippi and Missouri to the west.

These areas earned their names because as ocean waters began to rise and continued flowing inward and then receding, deposits of salt were left behind. This is an element that is essential to the diets of both humans and animals. Natural salt licks attract wildlife that will journey many miles providing them with the minerals they need.

Big Bone Lick, KY

The first thoroughfares used by the Delaware and Shawnee people and later frontiersmen were the results of generations of bison traveling through the forest and furrowing the prairies with trails. The first frontiersmen told stories about encountering herds of bison numbering in the thousands. It was the bison, huge in stature that wore deep trails, which became known as the Bison Trace Trail, leading to the many salt licks in Kentucky.

During the time when a huge sheet of ice began covering the ground stretching from Canada down to the Ohio region, animals were forced to move southward in search of food and water. Great herds of giant mastodons, wooly mammoths, ground sloths, saber toothed cats, bison, and giant stag moose were attracted to the warm salt springs that still bubble from the earth in Big Bone Lick State Park in Louisville, Kentucky. 38°53'13"N 84°44'52"W

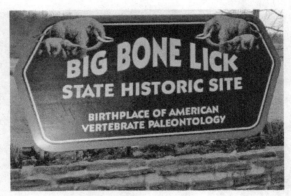

Big Bone Lick State Historical Site
© Cheryl L. Carter

Big Bone Lick Creek © Cheryl L. Carter

The Bison Trace Trail © Cheryl L. Carter

Unfortunately, some of the massive animals because of their weight got trapped in the marshy bog. Their boney remains sank into the soft, wet soil and many were preserved through a process called mineralization which may take hundreds to thousands of years. Bones that sank to the bottom of a bog and do not remain on the surface of the ground are most likely to be preserved as the temperature and humidity remain constant.

In 1739, Baron Charles de Longueuil was leading an expedition from Quebec to Louisiana where their trek took them down the Ohio River. They decided to stop for awhile and it was here they made the first discovery of prehistoric remains in the area. He found a forty inch femur at what is now known as Big Bone Lick. He also located a tusk big enough to fit into a barrel and three molar teeth; 6 1/2 pounds, 3 ¾ pounds and 15 inches round, and 1 ¾ pounds measuring 13 ½ inches round.

Baron Charles de Longueuil

In 1797, President Thomas Jefferson became the President of the American Philosophical Society. First on the agenda, was to "procure one or more entire skeletons of the Mammoth and other such unknown animals in the United States." Another reason for such an undertaking was that Jefferson had been highly influenced by the Age of Enlightenment, an intellectual and philosophical movement that dominated the world of ideas in Europe during the 18th century whose premise was to promote knowledge and science.

In May of 1803, President Jefferson sent Meriwether Lewis on an expedition down the Ohio River to meet up with Cincinnati physician William Goforth who had earlier conducted an excavation in which he discovered fossil remains of mammoth and mastodon. The expedition proved to be successful so in October, 1803, Lewis sent several specimens along with a letter describing Dr. GoForth's findings to President Jefferson.

Meriwether Lewis

Dr. William GoForth

There grew such an interest that in 1807 after the expedition was over, Jefferson convinced that there were still huge animals roaming the area, sent William Clark on another expedition to further excavate the area. This would be the first vertebra paleontology dig in the United States. Within a few weeks time they had discovered enough bones to fill three boxes. These were sent back to President Jefferson who in turn dedicated a room in the White House to some of the collection. Some were also sent to the National Institute of France in Paris, France.

From 1831-1848, there were many more digs as paleontologists and geologists explored the area. As a result, the Big Lick became included in many journals throughout the United States, France, England, and Germany.

Big Bone Lick, unique for its combination of salt springs and Late Pleistocene bone beds, became known as the Birthplace of American Vertebrate Paleontology. In 1972, it was listed on the National Registry of Historic Places, in 2002, the National Park Service designated it an official Lewis and Clark Heritage Trail Site, and in 2009, it was designated a Natural National Landmark by the United States Secretary of the Interior. Its excavation played a significant role in the development of scientific thought regarding extinction and the relationship of geology and paleontology the world over.

Big Bone Lick State Park is not only known for its fossils, but also for its paranormal activity. Here one might encounter an abundance of eerie sounds, disembodied whispers, and the cries of children lost in the woods who had been stolen by an evil spirit who was himself once murdered there. Natives once called the area "the land of the wild people" and with good reason for there have been an abundance of Bigfoot sightings reported throughout the years. Early settlers told stories of huge hairy men who threw rocks and tree limbs at them and stole their cattle. Even today, there are reports of Bigfoot walking along the side of the road and sometimes throwing rocks at unsuspecting passersby.

UFOs and the CSX Train

In 1997, there had been numerous reports of sightings of silver saucer shaped objects in the darkness of night. One mass sighting was on August 16, 2002, at 6:22 p.m. when eight UFOs were reported high in the evening sky. In 2012, a large triangular craft was observed for almost fifteen minutes.

There is a MUFON Report from a train engineer describing another bizarre incident. On January 14, 2002, at 2:47 a.m. a CSX train hauling coal was enroute to Louisville. The engineer recalled the exact time because his watch froze and to this day remains at that time. As they were approaching a bend, there appeared to be lights coming from around the other way. That usually indicated another train was coming and would pass on the opposite track. They turned off their lights so as not to blind the oncoming crew.

As they rounded the bend, the computer began to flash on and off, the speed recorder went crazy, both locomotives died, and alarms began to ring. Three objects hovered in the sky with what appeared to be search lights that were scanning the river. One hovered about 10-12 feet above the track. It was metallic silver, no windows, with multiple colored lights near the bottom and in the middle.

Depiction of the UFO colliding with the train

Because both engines were dead, when they rounded the corner they made little noise and the object did not respond in time. They hit it going about 30 mph with 16,000 tons trailing behind them. The object clipped the top of the lead engine and then skipped back slicing a chunk out of the trailing unit and the first two cars. After the impact, the other two objects disappeared. Luckily nobody onboard the train was injured.

Damage to the lead engine

Fortunately, the emergency brakes initiated due to loss of power and they stopped about a mile after the impact. They notified the dispatcher who told them to inspect the cars and see if they would be able to hold the rail. He then told them to go to a specific yard which was no longer in full operation.

They pulled into the yard around 5:15 a.m. and found it rather odd that the huge overhead lighting in the yard was dark. The only lights they saw were from what they thought were railroad officials parked near the end of the tracks. Suddenly, they heard vehicle doors slamming, men in dark attire began running toward them, and they saw lights glaring from all directions. The only thing they didn't see was railroad officials.

Men In Black

Someone who called himself Ferguson shook the engineer's hand and instructed him to follow them into the old yard office. Once they were inside, the men started to ask questions, hundreds of questions. They also informed the crew that for their own protection they would be medically tested before leaving. The engineer repeatedly asked to speak to his foreman and was repeatedly denied. Then they confiscated his conductor's cell phone.

Hours later, they were finally escorted outside again. Strangely enough, the two locomotives and two cars had now been removed from the rest of the train. The engineer assumed they were now parked four tracks over under a huge tent structure that was buzzing with activity. The crew was lead off the property and instructed that due to national security their silence on this matter would be greatly appreciated.

They were put into a railroad vehicle and taken to a place where railroad officials questioned them once more, ordered a drug test, and then released them to get some rest. Eight hours later, the crew was back to work on another train. As they took the same route and passed by the old yard, they never saw any sign of the engines, cars, tent, or people. The newspaper reported that there had only been a rock slide incident. Had the Men in Black made it look as though nothing had ever happened?

The Mantell Incident

The area around Pope Lick is known to be a bed of UFO activity. Since 1953, there have been hundreds of sightings along with silent black helicopters. The most famous sighting was known as the Mantell Incident. The event was among the most publicized early UFO incidents.

Captain Thomas Frances Mantell, Jr. age 25 earned a Distinguished Flying Cross for his efforts in the Normandy Invasion called Operation Overload or D-Day. After the war, he returned to his hometown of Louisville and joined the Air

National Guard. On January 7, 1948, at 1:45 p.m. the control tower at Fort Knox received a report of a southwest bound circular object in the sky. Several witnesses watched for an hour and twenty-five minutes as the object appeared to remain stationary in the sky.

Captain Thomas Mantell

P-51D Mustang

Three P-51D Mustang single-seat fighter bombers of C-Flight of the 165th Fighter Squadron led by Captain Mantell were currently in the air doing maneuvers when they were instructed to approach the craft. All the pilots reported that the object was metallic, a tremendous size, and going upward at 180 mph which was half their speed. They continued in steep pursuit reporting the object was now ascending upward at 360 mph. At that point, the tower told them to level off their altitude. At 3:10, two of the pilots abandoned their interception at 22,500 feet. However, Captain Mantell notified the tower that he intended to continue pursuit and was still climbing. At 3:15, the tower lost contact with him. Just minutes later, having reached well over 22,555 feet, he apparently blacked out from lack of oxygen. Witnesses watched as his plane began spiraling back towards the ground crashing upon impact. His watch stopped working at 3:18 p.m. the exact time of the crash.

The Mantell Incident was investigated by Project Sign the first Air Force research group assigned to investigate unidentified flying object reports. Project Blue Book considered it one of the three classic UFO cases of 1948 that would help define the UFO phenomenon. The other two cases were the Chiles-Whitted UFO Encounter in July 1948 in Montgomery, Alabama, and the Gorman Dogfight in October 1948 in Fargo, North Dakota. These cases would redefine the UFO phenomenon in the public mind and convince Air Force Intelligence Specialists that UFOs were real and could pose a threat.

Pope Lick Goat Man

Colonel Beauregard Schildknecht was the owner and ringmaster of a traveling circus that performed in the South during the 1930's. Although in the beginning he strived to provide entertainment, his name soon became synonymous with being a swindler. His carnies carried out the role of sideshow entertainers by day and malevolent cut throats by night. Unfortunately, instead of leaving happy memories behind, they left a series of unsolved thefts, missing people, and gruesome accidental deaths.

One night, the circus stopped in a small town near Beltsville, Maryland. Sometime during the night, Madame Bristelles, the Bearded Lady, discovered that someone had abandoned an infant in the crate of hay outside of her tent. As she reached down to pick up the child, she gasped at the sight before her; stubs protruding from its forehead and deformed legs with cloven hooves instead of feet. Nonetheless without hesitation, she quickly took the baby into her tent giving it some food and much needed comfort.

The following day when the Colonel saw its little deformed body, he immediately knew he had discovered just what he needed as the starring attraction for his Freak Show. He snatched the child from the arms of Madame Bristelles and raised it in captivity never again allowing it out of its cage. Over the years, the beast grew in size and strength and its stubs grew into full sized horns. When not on exhibit in the Freak Show, the Goat Man spent most of its life chained to the wall of a cage inside a circus train car. The carnies continuously whipped it into submission and the only food it was given were leftover scraps from the vendor's grease pit. There was no doubt that the beast began to develop a fury deep inside.

Pope Lick Goat Man

One night during a violent thunder storm, the circus train was passing through Fisherville, Kentucky, on its way to the next performance in Louisville. Suddenly a huge bolt of lightning struck the tracks causing the train to derail just ahead of the trestle over the Pope Lick Creek. Most of the carnies were instantly killed and many bodies lay beneath the twisted wreckage. It was said that body parts were mysteriously discovered as far away as two miles from the crash site.

The Goat Man survived and was at last finally free from the clutches of those who had tormented him for so many years. Had it been he who justifiably so took revenge on the survivors ripping them to shreds with his own bare hands? And what became of the Colonel whose body was never found? Some suspect he had somehow survived the wreck and fled. Or had the Goat Man captured him keeping him prisoner in a cave reciprocating the torture he had once endured?

Many believe the Goat Man never left. Perhaps he lives in an underground cave somewhere in the woods. However, this much is for certain, his inbred hatred of cruel humanity had made him extremely dangerous. Since then, there have been numerous sightings of the Goat Man and disturbingly many missing people, mysterious deaths, as well as deer and cattle mutilations. It is believed that he protects the trestle and those who dare to trespass into his domain have met their fate. Legend has it that he lures people to the top of the trestle by mimicking the sounds of a baby or even calling out their names. He then hypnotizes them keeping them frozen on the tracks as an oncoming train approaches.

The trestle rises ninety feet above the Pope Lick Creek, named after William Pope who used to own the property, stretching 772 feet across to the other side. It remains an active route for the Norfolk-Southern Railway with 15-20 heavily loaded freight trains traversing the tracks each day. And yet, there are people who don't realize this and foolishly scale an eight foot security fence to gain access to the trestle. The trestle at one time was equipped with platforms ensuring a pedestrian had an island of safety to run to should a train suddenly appear. They were removed to discourage people from walking up there, but obviously that didn't work. The Federal Railroad Administration estimates that ten people have died while trespassing and 16 others were injured.

Norfolk-Southern Railway Trestle

Security Fence and No Trespassing Sign

Among those are: In February 1987, Jack Charles Bahm age 17 was struck by an oncoming train. Three months later in May 1987, David Wayne age 19 died after he jumped trying to escape Bain age 26 was struck by an oncoming train. Her boyfriend Dane Knee age 41 managed to hold on until the train passed and climb back onto the tracks. On May 28,

2019, two 15 year old girls wanting to be cool climbed the trestle to the tracks. One died and another was seriously injured when they met with an oncoming train. In 2000, Nicholas Jewell age 19 fell to his death when he could no longer hold on as a train passed. Are there truly so many thrill seekers or is the Goat Man hungry for souls luring them into his kingdom?

French Lick

Likewise, the area around French Lick, once a French Trading post in 1811, has its own share of mysterious phenomenon. In the early 1800's, pioneer farmers spoke of a giant snake about 30-40 feet long, its body as wide as a barrel. They also talked about a huge hairy creature that would steal livestock and break into their cabins. In 1960, a similar strange hairy creature with glowing red eyes was seen several times. Locals named it "Florescent Freddy." During the 1970's huge Thunderbirds were seen in the Hoosier National Forest. Throughout the 1990's and continuing today Bigfoot and large footprints have also been sited there; at times their familiar yelp can be heard and at other times rocks are heard being thrown. In 1969, a farmer reported seeing a large hairy creature in his barnyard. He later made a cast of a large four-toed footprint. Strangely enough, the creature appeared right after several UFOs were seen overhead.

The Hoosier National Forest is located in the hills of Southern Indiana. The forest, managed by the United States Forest Service, occupies 202,814 acres, encompasses nine counties, and contains 300 miles of trails. In 1987, it was listed on the National Register of Historic Places.

Within the forest are numerous segments of the Buffalo Trace, the wilderness trail that was carved into the landscape by the migrating buffalo. It was this trail that pioneers followed leading them to places to homestead. Potts Creek flows about forty miles down the valley through Craig and Alleghany Counties. In 1767, the creek was named after John Potts who settled near the headwaters after journeying from Richmond, Virginia.

Deep within the forest along broken terrain, are the Potts Creek Rockshelters. They consist of a pair of shallow, cave-like openings encompassing 4,355 feet at the base of a bluff that were formed when the soft sandstone eroded away under the influence of the weather. Archeologists believe it was inhabited more than 10,000 years ago by the Archaic, Woodland, and Paleo people. The site is listed on the National Registry of Historic Places.

Potts Creek Rockshelter

In 1808 after the Civil War, Jonathan Lindley a successful lumber merchant in North Carolina heard about land in the Indiana Territory that was open for settlement. There were two factors that peaked his interest: The Midwest had vast untouched forests and the territory supported Emancipation. In addition, the Northwest Ordinance of 1787 simplified the process of securing land titles.

He and his son Zachariah journeyed west in hopes of finding a place they could establish a Quaker colony. Lindley purchased large tracts of land along the Wabash River, the Illini word for "water over white stones." Then he built a grist mill on Lick Creek in the upper limestone highlands. In 1811, he went back to North Carolina and returned with twenty families to join the settlement.

Eleven of the families were "free men" and Lumbee, a tribe from North Carolina. The free men were emancipated people who left North Carolina searching for the freedom they were being denied under the new restrictive Black Code devised to override their free status. Traveling with the Quakers and living deep within the forest assured their safety.

The Fugitive Slave Act of 1793 was a Federal law that was written to enforce Article 4 of the United States Constitution which required free states to return runaway slaves to their masters. On September 18, 1850, the Fugitive Slave Law was written to penalize officials who did not arrest alleged runaway slaves charging them $1000 each time. Officials were required to arrest them on only the word of a witness. The accused was not able to have a jury trial or speak in his own behalf. Anyone discovered offering food and shelter to runaways was subject to a $1000 fine and six months in prison.

In 1831, Mathew Thomas age 22 purchased eighty acres of land twenty miles from the Ohio River and began the Lick Creek Settlement for free men. Slavery was still legal in the states south of the Ohio River. The Lick Creek Settlement served as part of the Underground Railroad enabling fugitives to cross the Ohio River and into the safety of the forest. However, when the Indiana Constitution was adapted in 1851, free men were again under scrutiny when they were required to register with the state and pay a $500 cash bond to guarantee their good behavior. Even Mathew Thomas found himself seeking the aid of his Quaker friends who would vouch for his integrity.

With the Civil War in full force by the 1860's, the population of the Lick Creek Settlement began to decline. By 1862, most of those remaining left the settlement and moved farther north with many continuing on to Canada. Today, the only reminder that Lick Creek even existed is a long abandoned family cemetery; its limestone gravestones fallen, covered with moss as if nature is trying to reclaim the land. The only marker that was preserved said: Mathew Thomas, born April 2, 1817, died June 30, 1867.

Mathew Thomas grave

The Knights of the Golden Circle

The Hoosier National Forest was also where in 1863, the Hines Raid, a Confederate exploratory mission led by Captain Thomas Henry Hines took place. Well-known for his spying activity, he and his unit posed as Union soldiers with their mission being to prepare the way for Morgan's Raid, led by John Hunt Morgan of Kentucky, across the Ohio River and into Indiana. Disguised as a Union soldier he attempted to discover what support the Knights of the Golden Circle would provide.

Captain Thomas Henry Hines

The Knights of the Golden Circle was an underground fraternal order established on July 4, 1854 by George W. Brinkley. The main objective was to assimilate an extension of Southern interests such as slavery in a "golden circle" within a new Territory encompassing 2,400 miles of Central America, the Confederate States of the United States, and the Caribbean with Havana, Cuba being the center. They also proposed there be a separate confederation of slave states within the United States that were south of the Mason-Dixon line that would secede from the Union.

Jesse W. James and John Wilkes Booth were both members of the Knights of the Golden Circle. Booth's assassination of President Abraham Lincoln was an attempt to get Confederate prisoners freed.

George W. Brinkley   Symbol of the
Knights of the Golden Circle

Bigfoot in Hoosier National Forest

Although many who once lived deep within the forest are now a mere memory, there still remains an elusive being that enjoys the likes of the woods. People have reported rocks being thrown at them, vocalizations, and large foot prints. In fact, the Big Foot Researchers Organization (BFRO) says 78 reports have been filed in Indiana in the last five decades with many of these reports being actual sightings.

One such sighting occurred in February, 2019, by several credible witnesses. On that day, a bus with fifty church parishioners was on a field trip to the forest when they observed the ten foot tall, hairy creature. As the others looked on, Josh Hammer, an ex-Marine, exited the bus and attempted to approach the cryptid. During his tour in Vietnam, he had gained great experience sneaking up on people. Armed with only the knife that he always carried, he crept up upon the creature. Strangely enough as he got within forty feet of it, the Bigfoot appeared oblivious of him and the bus as it stood looking into the creek, cocking its head to the side, apparently admiring its reflection. Suddenly now aware that something was behind it, the Bigfoot turned and ran into the forest. Josh reported that the creature had a human-like face covered in hair.

The Stafford UFO Incident

On January 6, 1976, three good friends Mona Stafford, Louise Smith, and Elaine Thomas went to dinner at the Redwood Restaurant in Lancaster, Kentucky, to celebrate Mona's 36th birthday. At about 11:15, they headed home expecting to arrive around midnight. Louise had just turned off Highway 27 and onto Highway 87 when they noticed a bright red object in the night sky. At first, Mona was concerned thinking it might have been an airplane on fire heading for a crash landing.

Lexington Herald Leader
Louise Smith, Elaine Thomas, and Mona Stafford

As the object descended, it became apparent that it wasn't a plane. However, they weren't sure what it was, but it was enormous. The object was metallic, disc-shaped, a dome on the top, with a ring of red lights around the middle, and a yellow blinking light on the other side. Closer and closer it came when suddenly Louise realized she could no longer control the car. The vehicle began moving at a dangerous speed of 85 mph. She took her foot off the gas pedal and pushed down on the brake, but to no avail. Mona grabbed the wheel attempting to help, but the car was now out of their control. Who or what was in control was the furthest thing from their minds.

Now the strange object was getting closer. It began to follow them from behind and then flipped on its end flying close to the driver's side where it hovered for awhile. Then it moved ahead of them on the highway. Suddenly, a bluish-white light shot into the car lighting up the entire inside and filling the car with a sort of fog. Instantly, they felt a burning sensation so strong that they were unable to open their eyes.

Seconds later, the light had diminished, and they saw they were now on the outskirts of Houstonville eight miles from where they had just been. The ladies were quite shaken and all they wanted to do was forget this part of the evening and get home. Little did they know this was something they would never forget. No, not even if they tried.

Having finally arrived at Louise Smith's house, they thought this would be an opportunity for them to relax and attempt to make some sense of what had happened. Unfortunately, that was not the case. Once inside, they realized that this was much more than they could comprehend. They all had red, burning eyes, a strange red burn mark three inches long and one inch wide with clearly defined edges on the back of their necks, and burns on exposed skin. As Louise went into the bathroom and began taking off her watch so she could wash her hands, she noticed the minute hand was rapidly spinning around the dial. It was then that they glanced at the clock on the wall which showed 1:20 a.m. Now that was rather odd because how could it have taken over two hours to travel thirty-five miles? Thinking that the clock was malfunctioning they went over to the house of a neighbor named Lowell Lee. But when they got there, he confirmed the time to be correct.

Confused at what to do next, they decided it would be best to notify the police. The following day they also contacted the Navy Recruiting Station. However, neither one did anything to help them. The only thing the Navy did was leak some of the details to a Lexington tv station which, in turn, quickly reached the press where the Kentucky Advocate ran a story.

Strange things continued to occur the next few weeks. Mona's eyes worsened and she was diagnosed with severe conjunctivitis. Louis's parakeets were now terrified at the sight of her and one bird soon died. Her car began to develop mysterious electrical problems and when she touched the alarm clock it quit working. All three women were extremely exhausted for no apparent reason.

Word about the story reached Jerry Black of MUFON and Dr. Jseof Allen Hynek of CUFOS, the Center for UFO Studies and both men were very interested in interviewing the women. Dr. Hynek suggested that the women subject themselves to Hypnotic Regression. Upon being contacted, they were very hesitant about the men's desire to help them. They did not want their story to gain any more publicity. Therefore, they had no desire to discuss anything further and were under the impression that this would all pass in time. But it didn't.

Mona Stafford finding it exceedingly more difficult to perform her functions as a secretary, finally decided to try the regression session. On March 7, 1976, Dr. Ronald Leo Sprinkle a psychologist, hypnotherapist and former Professor at the University of Wyoming, performed the first session with Jeffery Black and Dr. Hynek observing.

In July 1976, Lexington Police Detective James C. Young agreed to administer separate polygraph tests to each of the women regarding their strange experience. The results of the tests determined that all three women believed they were telling the truth to the series of questions put before them. Moreover, the women were considered reliable and in good standing within the community as Mona Stafford, age 36, Elaine Thomas, age 48, and Louise Smith, age 44, were all active members of the Baptist Church.

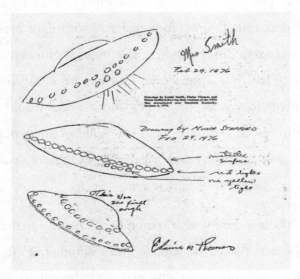

Elaine Thomas Drawings of the craft
February 29, 1976

Mona Stafford remembered being taken from the car. She was placed on a white table and noticed a bright white light or energy shining down on her that seemed to hold her down on the table so she could not move. A large eye was observing her. Four small humanoid figures about four feet tall surrounded the table as her body was being scanned and instruments were being used to apply pressure on her arms and legs. Some sort of warm liquid was applied to her face and body. She experienced great pain in her eyes and at one point it felt like they were pulled out.

Elaine Thomas recalled being taken from the vehicle. She was placed inside a small chamber with a window and watched as grey figures, four feet tall, with dark eyes walked back and forth observing her. The most frightening part was that they had put a device around her neck. Whenever she attempted to speak or think, the device would tighten, choking her as a punishment. A bullet-shaped object was placed over her heart which caused her extreme pain. Later she noticed a red spot in that area.

Louise Smith also remembered being lifted from the car. She was placed on a table and examined. Three beings, four foot tall, one with one eye, and the others with two, surrounded the table. They had no mouth and communicated by telepathy. A warm liquid was applied to her entire body. In the weeks following the abduction, she lost twenty-eight pounds. During the late summer of 1976, she had an uncontrollable desire to return to the site of the encounter. On August 1, she drove there, got out of her car, and heard a voice say, "Feel your hands." When she did so, she realized that the three rings which she always wore, a gold band, a pearl ring, and a gold band with a diamond and onyx were missing. On August 26, she walked out her front door to find the diamond and onyx band on the steps. As she bent over to pick it up, an overwhelming feeling came over her compelling her to walk to the nearby creek and throw it into the water.

Coincidently, there were several reports that night in neighboring towns about an unidentified flying object in the sky. The farmer who lived near the abduction site reported seeing a low flying object shoot down a white beam near a car at the same time as the incident.

Throughout the years UFO sightings in the Triangle began to amass and would continue to this day. Descriptions vary from silver oval shaped objects to black triangular crafts. Strangely enough, Bigfoot sightings seem to coincide with the same events. Could the creature be an alien entity? Or perhaps they are both able to travel back and forth into another dimension through a mysterious doorway.

Chapter 4
Bridgewater Triangle

Massachusetts is one of the original thirteen Colonies and the place where the Pilgrims arrived on the Mayflower. Massachusetts Bay Colony was named after the Massachusett people whose name is derived from the Wopanaah word "muswach sut" meaning "near the Great Hill."

East Bridgewater is the birthplace of Isaac W. Sprague, known as the "Living Skeleton" or the "Original Thin Man." He was born May 21, 1841, and was a completely normal child until the age of twelve. One day after swimming, he became ill and began to lose weight. At first the weight loss was of no concern, however when it continued his mother took him to the see a doctor, several in fact. The doctors were puzzled, but later diagnosed him as having extreme progressive muscular atrophy which caused his body to lose fat and muscle mass. As an adult, he worked with his father as a cobbler, but soon as his condition worsened, he became so weak that he was unable to stand for long periods of time making it impossible for him to perform his duties. In 1865 when he was 24, he was spotted by a carnival promoter who offered him a job in the side show. At first being a bit insulted he refused the offer, but then realized that he could make a living capitalizing on his appearance. Later that year, he was introduced to Phineas Taylor Barnum who paid him $80 a week to be part of his Barnum's American Museum. In 1868, he barely escaped with his life as the museum burned to the ground. A few years later, he and his wife escaped another fire when the Newhall House burned down. Sadly only six months later, he died at age 44 weighing a mere forty-three pounds.

Isaac W. Sprague

Charles Sherwood Stratton was born on January 4, 1838. At birth he weighed in at a healthy nine pounds eight ounces. As a child he seemed to develop normally until at the age of six months when he stopped growing at two feet six inches. Doctors determined that he would not grow any more. The exact cause was not known as x-rays were not invented until 1895 and the medical techniques of the time were limited. When he was four years old, a distant cousin P.T. Barnum asked if he could be part of his American Museum to which his father happily agreed. So in 1842, Charles was renamed General Tom Thumb after the fictional character in the 17th century book "Tom Thumb." In the story, a Wizard named Merlin granted a childless woman's wish of being happy to have a son even if he were no larger than her husband's thumb. Barnum paid him $25 per week to perform in his show. For three years they toured Europe and even performed for Queen Victoria.

P. T. Barnum and Tom Thumb

For centuries, the 200 square mile area located just south of Boston, Massachusetts known as the Bridgewater Triangle has been known as a place of the unusual and unexplained. The boundaries begin at Rehoboth, extends north to Abington, south to Freetown, and back up to Rehoboth with Bridgewater located in the dead center. Strange as these stories are, they pale in comparison to the wealth of interest and intrigue that lie within the confines of the Triangle. Among them are various paranormal phenomena including Native curses, Thunderbirds, Giant Snakes, Bigfoot, and UFOs.

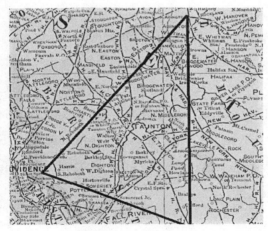

Bridgewater Triangle

The Freetown-Fall River Forest, situated in the center of the Bridgeport Triangle, is located at Freetown and Fall River, Massachusetts with the bulk of it running through Freetown. The forest of 5,441 acres with 50 miles of unpaved roads and trails is a favorite of hikers, fisherman, and hunters in the summer and cross-country skiers and dog sledders in the winter. The forest and surrounding land was the home of the Wampanoag Nation, the "People Of the First Light," for almost ten thousand years and now includes their 227 acre Watuppa Reservation. It was the Wampanoag people who taught the Pilgrims of Plymouth Colony how to survive that first winter.

According to the Wampanoag lore, there was a friendly giant named Maushop. He was a beloved god who was thought to be responsible for the creation of Cape Cod. He would often fish bare-handed for whales in Popponesset Bay. One day he emptied the sand from his giant moccasins into the water creating the islands of Martha's Vineyard and Nantucket.

Oil Painting of Maushop © Stan Murphy

The forest is also said to be the home to a race of diminutive humanoid creatures known as Pukwedgies. They are thought to be the oldest mystical creatures in North America whose name means "person of the wilderness." These creatures are described as being troll-like beings about two to three feet tall. They have human-like features except for enlarged noses, ears and fingers. Their skin is smooth grey and sometimes glows.

Pukwedgies

They once lived alongside the giant Maushop, but soon felt forgotten as they realized they were not revered as was the friendly giant. Feeling unappreciated, they instead turned into tricksters and began to do misdeeds. Some even believe they conspired to kill the giant because he suddenly disappeared. According to Native lore, Pukwedgies can appear and disappear in an instant, shapeshift, shoot poison arrows and create fire at will. They are known to steal children, attack people with spears, and push people off cliffs. There have been several mysterious suicides at a ledge in the forest. Some believe it was not suicide, but rather that their misfortune may have been linked to the Pukwedgies.

Hockomock Swamp
Chief Metacon

Hockomock Swamp, the largest freshwater swamp in Massachusetts, consists of 6,000 acres of black rivers, marshes, ponds, thickets of cedar and maple trees, beds of brush, twisting vines, sinkholes and quicksand. It stretches across parts of Easton, Bridgewater, Norton, Raynham, Taunton and West Bridgewater, crossed by a number of roads including Route 24 and 138 and an old railroad bed.

Hockomock Swamp

The Algonquian called it "the place where spirits dwell." The Wampanoag believed that Hockomock, the chief deity of death and disease, dwells within the swamp where he keeps the souls of the dead. Moreover, for the last 8,000 years, they avoided the area except to use it as a sacred burial ground believing it was a passageway to another world. Something about the swamp struck terror into the hearts of the Puritan colonists and they called it the "Devil's Swamp."

The area surrounding the swamp was the site of the King Philip's War one of the most costly wars of resistance in New England history. The war lasting from 1675-1676 is named after Chief Metacom of the Wampanoag Tribe who, like his father Massasoit, the Grand Sacken, took on the English name of Philip to show his alliance with the colonists. As the Grand Metacon, Chief Massasoit served as an intertribal leader maintaining harmonious social relations among a confederation of Algonquian Tribes, the Wampanoag, Narragansett, and Pokanoket, and the Mayflower pilgrims. After his father's death, Metacom became the Grand Sacken and the settlers called him King. Through the years, Metacom's dignity and steadfastness impressed the colonists. However, there came a point in which his power also frightened them and they soon deemed him as someone they could not control.

Chief Massasoit "King Philip"

John Sassmon was an Indian who converted to Christianity commonly known as a Praying Indian that lived in a Christianized Native settlement or Praying Town. He was instrumental as a mediator negotiating with both the Indians and colonists while not belonging to either party. He began serving as a translator and advisor to Metacom, but soon became a tribal informer for the colonists.

On January 29, 1675, he secretly contacted the governor Josiah Winslow concerning the impending attack by King Philip. However, the governor not fully convinced with the validity of the information was slow to act. On January 29, John Sassmon's body was discovered where it had slipped beneath the ice of the Assawompset Pond. At first the colonists believed he had fallen into the water while fishing, but later examination determined his neck had been broken with great force.

On June 8, 1675, three of Wampanoag warriors were executed by Plymouth authorities for the murder of John Sassmon. Some members of the Wampanoag tribe felt the trial wrongly accused the three men and retaliated by attacking the town. On June 21, 1675, the colonists, fearing for their safety, prepared to negotiate with King Philip. However, King Philip stood steadfast in tribal beliefs and was not about to be forced to recognize English sovereignty. On June 24 according to Increase and Cotton Mather, as parishioners were walking out of church after the

Midsummer Day mass in Swansea, the Wampanoag ambushed and killed several colonists. This marked the beginning of the conflict as the Wampanoag used tribal alliances with the Narraganset, Nipmuc and Pocumtuc to coordinate efforts to push the colonists out of New England. In return, the English joined by the Mophegans and Mohawks retaliated by destroying native villages.

In 1676, as the colonists numbers increased, King Philip and some followers took refuge in the Assawompset Swamp area in southern Massachusetts. A group of rangers led by Captain Benjamin Church located them in the Misery Swamp near Mount Hope.

On August 12, 1676, King Philip met his demise when he was fatally shot by John Alderman a Praying Indian. It is said that as he lay dying in the mud, he called out a curse upon the land that had been taken from his people. Alderman beheaded him and sold his severed head to Plymouth Colony authorities for thirty shillings, the standard rate for Indian heads. King Philip's head was mounted on a spiked pole at the entrance to Plymouth, Massachusetts where it remained for two decades. His body was quartered and hanged in trees. Alderman was given King Philips right hand as a trophy. Some Wampanoags later stole the skull form the Fort and took it to a secret place. To this day, many take the journey to this place. According to tribal legend, the skull speaks to those most worthy.

The King Philip's War was the bloodiest war per-capita in American history. Over 3,000 Native men, woman, and children were either killed or sold to slave ships bound for the West Indies. After his death, King Philip's own wife and nine year old son were captured and sold as slaves.

Anawan Rock

Anawan Rock, a large dome of conglomerate rock, coarse-grained sedimentary rock composed of gravel, sand and clay, twenty-five feet tall and seventy-five feet wide, is located in the Hockomock Swamp just off U.S. Route 44, Rehoboth, Massachusetts. In 1983, it was added to the National Register of Historic Places. It is named after Chief Anawan, the War Chief of Chief Metacome who on this spot on August 28, 1676, surrendered to the colonists ending the King Philip War. Legend has it that warrior spirits haunt the area and "ghost fires" or spectral lights hover over the rock at night.

Anawan Rock

Profile Rock

Profile Rock, a fifty feet high granite rock formation is located on Old Joshua's Mountain near the Freetown Forest in Freetown, Massachusetts. The mountain was named after the first settler Joshua Tisdale.

Many believe the rock depicts the likeness of Chief Massasoit. It was at this place that the Wampanoag met to meditate and discuss tribal issues. Legend has it that ghostly warriors can be seen dancing around the rock at night.

Profile Rock

Dighton Rock

Dighton Rock, near Berkley, Massachusetts, is a forty ton grey-brown crystalline sandstone boulder this area that arrived to the Taunton River by means of the melting glaciers during the last Ice Age. The slanted, six-sided, five feet high and eleven feet long boulder contains a mass of ancient carvings or petroglyphs of unknown origin across one of the six sides. It contains a trapezoidal face and is inclined seventy degrees to the northwest facing the water looking towards the

Grassy Island burial grounds, an 8,000 year old Native site. When archaeologists opened the graves, the red ochre a clay pigment used in burials to represent the return to earth as a form of ritual rebirth, covering the bodies disappeared. Strangely enough, the film used to take photographs at the excavation would not develop.

Dighton Rock

In 1963, the boulder was removed from the water and displayed in the Dighton Rock State Park Museum. In 1980, it was placed on the National Registry of Historical Places. The exact origin of the carvings is unknown, but there have been several theories. It was first discovered in 1680 by Reverend John Danford who attributed the carvings to be the work of Natives, most likely the Wampanoag. In 1689, Reverend Cotton Mather described the rock in a sermon saying it had a certain undesirable feeling about it and was most likely created by Satanist who had arrived before the Pilgrims. George Washington, in 1786, agreed with Danforth's theory as he had also seen similar carvings in Virginia. In 1837, Danish writer Charles Christian Rafn concluded the inscriptions were Viking. Despite all the claims, the carvings have yet to be deciphered.

Solitude Stone

Solitude Stone is located near Forest Street in West Bridgewater just before the wooden bridge. For years, it was hidden beneath a layer of dirt and moss. That was until that day of August 4, 1916, when twenty-seven year old Evelyn Packard disappeared. She took the trolley from her Brockton home to the Americanage Club and rented a canoe. Within an hour of her renting the canoe, she vanished. Two boys later found her coat and a pillow inside the dry canoe with no signs that anything had gone awry. Authorities believed she had wandered into the Hockomock Swamp and had become disoriented. One newspaper headline even stated, "Doctors Fear Girl Is Crazed In Hockomock Swamp." Her body was found three days later under the Skim Milk Bridge that was two bridges down from the Comfort Bridge.

SEARCHING FOR MISS PACKARD

Mystery Deepens at West Bridgewater

Young Woman May Be Lying Ill or Dead in Woods

Special Dispatch to the Globe
WEST BRIDGEWATER, Aug 4—
Search was this morning renewed for
Miss Evelyn E. Packard, daughter of
John D. Packard of Brockton, who so

Boston Daily Globe
August 5, 1916

AUGUST 5, 1916 **   *Copyrighted.*

TRACE GIRL TO TANGLED SWAMP

Searchers Find Footprints Resembling Those of Miss Packard Leading Into Morass

SCHOOLBOYS SEARCHING FOR MISSING GIRL CANOEIST.

118

During one of the searches, a reporter took a break and sat down on the nearby Comfort Bridge, a bridge constructed of three immense stones. He looked down and noticed what appeared to be words on the flat stone supporting the south side of the bridge along with the Roman Numerals "MDCCCXII" or 1862. Upon the oblong shaped six foot stone were six lines:

"All ye, who in future days walk by Nunckatessett, stream love not him who hummed his lay cheerful to the parting beam, but the beauty that he wooed."

Solitude Stone

It was determined that this inscription was carved into the rock by Reverend Timothy Otis Paine of the New Church of Jerusalem. This is a religion based on Christianity and the teachings of the occultist Emanuel Swedenburg largely based on the eleven principles of the Age of Aquarius: Revolution, Evolution, Unity, Friendship, Transparency, Magic, Comedy, Abundance, Electricity, Brilliance and Freedom. Likewise, from the teachings came the Rite of Swedenburg, a fraternity that paralleled Freemasonry.

Reverend Otis Paine

Assonet Ledge

Assonet Ledge often times known simply as The Ledge, is a granite cliff looking down on an eighty foot deep rock quarry. It is not a natural formation, but instead, it is what remains of the area after being carved out by the Fall River Granite Company.

The area has long been associated with a range of very strange phenomena. Visitors have reported being overcome with a sudden sense of dread and foreboding when near the quarry and numerous suicides have been reported.

Assonet Ledge "The Ledge"

It has been rumored that it is an area frequented by Satanists as there have been several gruesome murders linked to Satanic rituals. Over a dozen confirmed homicides were reported from 1978-1979. In addition, some local graves have been desecrated and skulls stolen which were later found in the forest. Many cattle and goat mutilations have been linked to cult sacrifices. Or were they?

Extra-Terrestrials

The Ledge is also famous for UFO sightings. The first documented sighting took place on May 10, 1760. At 10:00 in the morning, a large sphere of fire was observed in the sky that cast shadows in bright sunlight. In 1908, two undertakers were driving a carriage from West Bridgewater to the center of Bridgewater when shortly after 3:00 a.m. they witnessed a strange object in the night sky. They described it as an unusually bright lantern about two and a half feet in diameter. They watched for about forty minutes as it appeared to hover at times and to keep a straight steady course at other times.

Dozens of other sighting were reported through the 1960's. One such sighting in 1974 was reported by then Governor Ronald Regan as he was flying over the Ledge with pilot Air Force Colonel Bill Paynter and two security personnel. They spotted a strange light tailing the plane that appeared to accelerate, decelerate and become elongated all within the space of a few minutes. It then suddenly shot up at a forty-five degree angle at a high rate of speed and disappeared.

On March 23, 1979, Jerry Lopes and Steve Sbraccia newsmen from WHDH channel 7 in Boston were leaving work and driving to the Raynham Dog Racing Track not far from the Hockomock Swamp. As they approached the junction of Route 24 and 106 in Taunton, they observed a strange object in the evening sky. They described it as being similar to a home plate with a bright light on the front. Jerry Lopes, having served 4 ½ years in the Air Force, indicated that the object was not a plane. It was however, the size of three 707's wing to wing. Many others had pulled their vehicles to the side of the road and watched while this object flew overhead. This mass-sighting became known as the Bridgewater Incident.

In November 1997, a police officer working the night shift in Bridgewater saw a very large triangular object with three white and two red star-like lights. On December 10, 1998 a witness near Route 44 saw a strange brightly lit craft with numerous red, green and white lights maneuvering over Assawompsett Pond in Middleboro. The object split into two and then they both flew geometric patterns at a high speed around in the sky displaying spectacular colored lights. The crafts then converged back into one and disappeared. Black helicopters were seen over the pond immediately following the incident as if searching for something.

Reports of unidentified objects in the sky continued. In 2011, twenty-one reports were filed when multiple witnesses spotted glowing balls or "ghost lights" in the night sky. September 2014, a diamond shaped craft was observed in the evening sky. On October 19, 2015, wing-shaped lights were seen "falling down" from the night sky.

Hockomock Swamp Cryptids

Cryptozooligical mysteries abound mostly in the Hockomock Swamp. A tall hairy seven foot creature standing upright has been seen entering, creeping along the swamp edges and disappearing. On April 8, 1970, two policemen had a strange encounter when their parked car suddenly began to lift off the ground. It felt as though someone was lifting the rear of the vehicle. One of the officers pointed a spotlight in that direction. What they saw illuminated in the light was a massive bear-like man. When it looked into the light, it ran away. People began calling this creature the Hockomock Swamp Monster.

One cold morning in 1978, Joseph DeAndrade saw a strange creature walking down a hill about 200 feet ahead of him. It was six feet tall, about 400 pounds, and covered with long brown fur.

On a cold night in 1980, John Barker, a trapper was in his canoe running trap lines. He became aware that something was watching him. He could hear the sound of the ice in the swamp cracking as whatever it was got closer. He turned to see what he described as a shadowy, hair-covered giant that smelled like a skunk, musty and dirty liked it lived in the dirt.

Other strange animals are said to live deep within the swamp. There have been several sightings of a huge black prehistoric-looking Thunderbird with a wingspan of between eight and twelve feet that were first seen in 1971. In 1984, there was a report of two of these creatures fighting each other as they flew over some trees. Again in 1992, there was s sighting of a bird with a ten to twelve foot wingspan flying overhead.

In 1976, a man on a nearby farm watched as a huge Phantom Dog with red glowing eyes ripped open the throats of two of his ponies. The dog was almost as big as the ponies.

The Purity Distilling Company Disaster

The North End, one of Boston's busiest neighborhoods was once a bustling port, the site of the North End Paving Yard, the Purity Distilling Company, and the Atlantic Avenue Elevated Railway. Just up the street was the Old North Church where one evening in 1775, lanterns were hung warning Paul Revere that the British troops were coming.

The Purity Distilling Company was a subsidiary of U.S. Industrial Alcohol, an alcohol distiller. Purity constructed in 1915, was responsible for keeping up the demand for munitions manufacturing during WWI because the United States, England, and France purchased the industrial alcohol in order to make dynamite and other explosives.

The harbor side facility at 529 Commercial Street contained a huge tank in which to offload molasses from ships arriving from Cuba, Puerto Rico, and the West Indies. Here it was stored until the time came to transfer it via pipeline to their Purity plant in Cambridge where it would be turned into industrial alcohol.

After WWI ended at the 11th hour on the 11th day of the 11th month in 1918, the facility focused entirely on producing alcohol for liquor. The tank measured fifty feet high, ninety feet across, and was capable of holding 2.5 million gallons. It was never filled to capacity except for that day on January 14, 1919, when a ship from Puerto Rico dropped off 2.3 million gallons topping off the tank as the facility attempted to keep up with the demand for grain alcohol as Prohibition neared passage.

Purity Distilling Company
529 Commercial Street

The day was January 15, 1919, and just four months ago, the Boston Red Sox won the World Series with a 23 year old pitcher named George Herman "Babe Ruth."

Boston Evening Globe (only 1¢) – September 11, 1918

Two days ago the temperature had only been two degrees, but this day was looking beautiful with an unseasonable temperature of 40 degrees. Workers at the Boston & Worcester freight terminal were loading freight train cars for the Union Freight Railroad that was located near the tank. Three children Antonio di Stasio age 8, his sister Maria age 10, and Pasquale Iantosca age 10 were also nearby gathering firewood for their families.

Around 12:30 p.m. there came a strange sound from the tank. By now most people had become accustomed to hearing it creak and moan. However, there was something different about the sound that day; something that just didn't seem right.

Suddenly, the rivets holding the bottom of the tank shot out making a sound like a machine gun. The tank exploded giving way to a massive wave of molasses that swept away the freight cars and blew out the doors and windows of nearby buildings. Witnesses said they felt the ground rumble and heard a loud roar as the tank collapsed.

Instantly, 2.5 million gallons of molasses traveling 35 mph because of the intense kinetic energy produced by the pressure engulfed the waterfront like a black tidal wave, 25 feet high, and 160 feet wide sweeping away people, freight cars, and the nearby Engine 31 Firehouse. The wave had such power that it drove steel panels from the tank against the support beams of the Atlantic Avenue Elevated railway knocking it down.

The massive wave of destruction was not discriminating as it made its way down Commercial Street obliterating everything in its path killing 21 and seriously injuring 150 others. Many died as the result of crushing and suffocation. Sadly, the three children were among those who did not survive. Minutes later as the molasses flooded the street its consistency began to change turning it into a very thick tar-like substance devouring everything in its path. Twenty-one minutes later, the wave had become calm. The only sounds that were heard were of the people and horses now buried within the waist high black muck. Rescuers had an arduous task as they quickly discovered that they too were being pulled into the sticky murkiness. Later that evening, temperatures again dropped below freezing which hindered the rescuers because the consistency of the molasses increased by a factor of four.

Boston Daily Globe - January 16, 1919

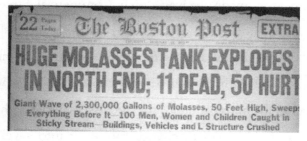

Boston Post – January 16, 1919

Mass destruction of the town

There were numerous factors that contributed to this disaster. It began with Arthur Jell treasurer of USIA becoming the manager of the project. He had no prior technical, architectural, or engineering experience which in turn, resulted in him taking many shortcuts during the construction. It was discovered that the steel walls of the tank ranged from .67 inches at the bottom to .31 at the top making them too thin to support the weight of a tank of molasses filled to capacity. The steel had been mixed with too little manganese resulting in a high transition capability making the metal brittle when it cooled below 59 degrees. There was a flawed rivet design and stress was too high on the rivet holes. Stress on the tank is directly related to the fluid inside. Molasses is 1.5 times heavier than water making it denser. It was apparent this particular type of tank was designed to hold water and not molasses.

There were signs of trouble from the very beginning. During the initial testing of the tank for leaks, Arthur Jell only filled the tank with six inches of water. When the facility actually began to fill the tank with molasses, it began to leak. When employees notified him of the situation, he merely had the blue steal painted brown so as to camouflage the leaking molasses.

All these factors were only compounded when the shipment of 2.3 million gallons of warm molasses from Puerto Rico was added to the tank of molasses that had been sitting in a temperature of two degrees the night before. Consequently, as the warm mixed with the cold, it triggered a fermentation process which produced gas. The workers even reported hearing the tank whining and groaning before the disaster.

Even though Boston had seven daily newspapers, the story of the Great Molasses Flood made front page news outranking the Prohibition Amendment.

Boston Daily Globe – January 16, 1919
Prohibition Amendment article below the Explosion Story

Chapter 5
Coudersport Triangle

Pennsylvania is one of America's thirteen Colonies, the home of the Liberty Bell, and where the Declaration of Independence and Constitution were signed. It was the birthplace of many notable people. Benjamin Franklin was one of the Founding Fathers of the United States. Edward Abbey was an author and essayist of such works as "Desert Solitaire" and "The Monkey Wrench Gang." Harry Alonza Longabaugh "the Sundance Kid" was an outlaw and member of Butch Cassidy's Wild Bunch. These outlaws were responsible for the longest string of successful train and bank robberies in American history.

This is also the home to strange phenomena. In the northern part of Pennsylvania is an area known as the Coudersport Triangle. It comprises several counties: McKean in the west, east to Potter and Tioga, south to Lycoming, west to Clinton, north to Cameron, and back to McKean and overlaps the mysterious Black Forest.

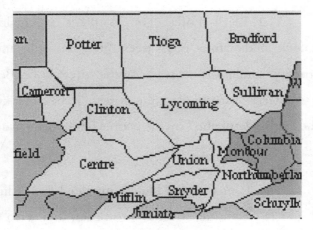

Coudersport Triangle

The Black Forest

The Black Forest

The Black Forest got its name when long ago, hemlock and white pine trees grew so tall and dense restricting sunlight from reaching the forest floor. Because of the mysteries surrounding the forest, it became known as "The Forbidden Land" by the people who once resided in the area.

The Pennsylvania Dutch migrated here during the 17th and 18th centuries. Contrary to belief, they were German, not Dutch. The language they spoke was a Deutsch dialect thus the misconception about their origin. They were mainly Amish, Mennonites, German Reformed, and Moravian. It was these people who first encountered a strange cryptid in the forest. It was a four foot tall, man-ape creature with reddish-brown hair. They named it Albatwitch from the word "alb" meaning "elf" and "witschen" for "quick gliding movement." Today, the creature can still be seen sitting in the trees or frequenting its favorite place, Chickies Rock which is an outcropping of trees that stands 100 feet above the waters of the Susquehanna River. The Susquehannock people once lived near the river and used the area as a burial ground. Strange sounds, almost like the crack of tree limbs, can be heard from the rock. Chickie Rock was also used as an observation point during the Civil War to observe Confederate soldiers who had made it that far before leading up the Battle of Gettysburg on July 1, 1863.

Albatwitch Sketch © Timothy Renner

Chickies Rock

The Algonquian people spoke of a Great Thunderbird who got its name because the flapping of its powerful wings sounded like thunder and lightning would flash from its eyes. Legend says that one day the Miami, from the Ojibwa word "Omaumeg," meaning "people of the peninsula," were at battle with their enemy the Mestchegamies. A great Thunderbird appeared and swooped down snatching a Miami Chief in its talons and flying away with its prey. Thinking that the Great Spirit had sent the Thunderbird to help their enemies, the Miami retreated and never returned. The Mestchegamies were victorious, but the victory was short lived. Now that the Thunderbird had gotten a taste of human flesh, it wanted more. So in order to appease it the Mestchehamies were forced to sacrifice some of their own people to satisfy its appetite.

The earliest documented sighting was that of Mrs. Elvira Coats in 1840. For the past twenty years they have been seen in the southern edge of the forest, north of Susquehanna River, between Pine Creek at the east, and Kettle Creek at the west. It was dark brown or black, had a wing span measuring twenty feet, and at rest on the ground was estimated to be eight feet tall.

Legend says there is a creature called the Squonk that lives within the forest. It is pig-like with saggy skin that is covered with warts. Because it is ashamed of the way it looks, the sad creature spends its days hiding and crying. Anyone attempting to capture the Squonk discovers that it is capable of dissolving into a pool of tears in order to escape. There was a man named J.P. Wentling who claimed to have captured the creature with a gunny sack. However, as he began to walk home, the heavy sack started to feel lighter. He stopped to take a look inside, but all he found was a wet bag.

Thunderbird

Squonk

The Triangle is also a known hot spot for Bigfoot sightings and vocalizations. One such encounter according to a report with BFRO, the Bigfoot Field Researchers Organization, happened in October, 1996. Three hunters were camping one night. Around 1:00 a.m. they heard the hoot of an owl and just for fun decided to hoot back. Suddenly, they heard a crashing sound in the brush followed by howling. It was too dark to determine what it was, but soon they heard ape-like inhaling and exhaling hoots as the creature began to circle the camp. By now the owl was quiet as if it sensed danger. This continued for about twenty minutes and then everything went silent. In the morning, they discovered broken tree limbs and six footprints in the mud circling the camp. Two footprints were significant enough to show detail of toe impressions. The footprints measured sixteen inches long and six inches wide.

Moores Run Disaster

Moores Run located just south of Coudersport was the site of the worst forest fire in Pennsylvania history that became known as the Moores Run Disaster. On May 11, 1891, Superintendent Badger and a train load of seventy-eight men set out from Austin to help fight a huge forest fire. They worked along Sinnemahoning Valley where they dug ditches, piled up dirt, and lighted backfires hoping to keep the fire contained. However, their efforts were in vain as the fire continued to spread with a vengeance. Forced to retreat, the men boarded the train hoping to move to a safe location.

Unfortunately, they soon found themselves in dire straits with the forest fire behind them and a huge skid of burning logs ahead of them. The engineer and Badger decided their only choice was to rush past the logs. The engineer wrapped a wet cloth around his face and wool around his arms. The men jumped into the cars and gathered in groups with some of them lying face down on the floors.

When they approached the flaming skid of logs, the heat became so unbearable that the men had to cover their mouths with a cloth in order to breathe. Just opposite the logs where the fire and heat was the most intense, the engineer decided to pull the throttle wider in hopes of escaping quicker. However, he had forgotten that the intense heat would spread the rails. Suddenly, the engine lurched and the entire train toppled over into the blazing fire.

The tumbled over cars quickly caught fire. For an instant, the men inside did not know what happened because they had their faces covered. When they finally realized their plight, they quickly scrambled to escape the cars hoping to find safety on the tracks if only for a short time.

The engine and entire train were destroyed in the fire. Six men died including the engineer and Badger, thirty-five were injured, thirty-four were dangerously burned, and seven remained missing. Most of the men were saved only because of their quick thinking to jump into the water below.

By the time the fire had burned itself out 48 hours later, 12 miles of timberland, 40,000,000 hemlock logs and timber were destroyed. Today, there is no evidence of the disaster. But some people say if you listen closely, you can still hear the lost men yelling for help.

The Dam That Could Not Break

About ten miles from Coudersport situated in a valley surrounded by hills covered with pine, hemlock and cherry, is the town of Austin. The Freeman Run Valley was known for its prosperity in the lumber industry and also for its resilience. On May 31, 1889, the valley flooded. In 1890, a fire destroyed a large portion of the town as it swept both sides of Main Street burning 43 businesses and a few family dwellings. The town rebuilt only to have a fire destroy the boarding house in the fall of 1891. Austin pushed forward rebuilding once again until in May 1894, the valley experienced yet another flood. Unfortunately in the fall of 1897, a massive fire swept through Main, Railroad, and Turner Streets destroying several stores, a theater, two churches, two boarding houses, and the homes of 89 families. And yet through all the hardships, Austin persevered.

Austin

When the old growth timber was exhausted, saw mills were replaced by paper mills. In 1900, George C. Bayless of New York chose Austin as the site of the Bayless Pulp and Paper Company and it soon became the largest mill in the area. By 1909, Bayless came to realize that the original earthen dam was too inadequate for his business needs. He hired engineer T. Chalkey Hatton to construct a larger dam across the valley that would supply water for the mill.

George Bayless

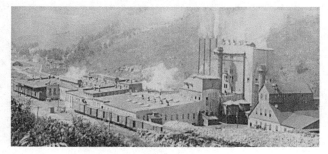

Bayless Pulp and Paper Company - 1900

Austin Dam

As part of their business agreement, Hatton was given two objectives: Construct a dam that was capable of holding a 200 million gallon reservoir and complete the project within a budget of $85,000. He further indicated that instead of using a 30 foot thick concrete, he would settle for a cheaper 20 foot thickness. As the construction neared completion, it became evident that the cost would be over budget. Bayless dissatisfied with the findings, pressured Hatton to make alterations in order to reduce the cost. However, Hatton informed him that the demands would violate sound engineering practice and advised him stay with the original proposal.

The dam was being constructed with cyclopean concrete that consisted of boulder-sized pieces of sandstone rock bound with concrete. Twisted steel rods were placed two feet apart to reinforce the dam. Bayless insisted that in order to reduce costs a minimal amount of iron rods be used to secure the dam to the foundation rock. He also contended that the outlet pipe be fitted with a wooden bulkhead instead of a valve.

Hatton was hesitant, however he had no alternative but to comply. All the discussion over changes put the project behind schedule and winter was approaching as they hurried the concrete construction. Finally on December 1,

1909, the dam was completed. It was fifty feet in height, extended 540 feet across the valley, and retained 250 million gallons of water.

On January 17, 1910, rain combined with warm temperatures that caused the snow to melt contributed to a sharp rise in the reservoir's level. A portion of the bottom earthen embankment slid down eight feet causing water to bypass the dam. The dam bowed 36 feet under the pressure of all the water it was retaining and the concrete started to crack. Had the dam a release valve as was in the original plans, the mill workers would have been able to release some water, but such as it was they were unable to remove the wooden cap as it was removable only during low flow conditions. Instead in a desperate attempt to relieve the pressure, workers set off dynamite to blast a notch eight feet wide along the crest.

Concerned with the thought of the dam failing and the fact it was less than a mile downstream, the townspeople fled to the safety of higher grounds. Remarkably, the quick thinking efforts of the mill workers succeeded in containing the water. Hatton consulted with Edward Wegman an expert of gravity design and developed a repair plan. Bayless contended that the dam was safe as is and refused their help.

The residents returned to their homes after being reminded the mill had "the dam that could not break," but soon discovered there was something unsettling. A stranger, a tall man dressed entirely in black began to appear and disappear along the Buffalo & Susquehanna Railroad tracks. Railroad workers witnessed the man sometimes riding inside the passenger cars. Other times he was seen lurking about the tracks or crawling between and running over the tops of the cars. Who or what was this mysterious man in black? Why was he there? There wasn't anyone brave enough to ask.

Mysterious Man in Black

The sightings continued for a year until the day of September 30, 1911. It began as a typical Saturday, but soon the residents would come to realize there was nothing typical about that day. At 2:15 from her house on the hill outside of town, Cora Brooks was sitting on her porch admiring the beautiful day. Decent people didn't say her name unless it was a whisper about the brothel on the hill.

Cora Brooks and her house on the hill

Suddenly, she heard the dam quake under pressure. She hurriedly notified the town below and alarms were sounded. But since there had been recent false alarms, many people didn't pay much attention to the warning.

Within fifteen minutes, a massive wave of water hit Austin; raging water that carried with it 20,000 cord feet of pulpwood from the remains of Bayless Mill upstream. The force of the water destroyed almost everything in its path. Gas mains severed causing fires to erupt and spread throughout the town. Seventy-eight people lost their lives that day. Tragic as it was, it may have been a lot more had it not been for the quick thinking of Cora Brooks, the name that everyone proudly spoke.

This was the worse dam failure in United States history and the second worse flood disaster in Pennsylvania history. This event inspired legistration to take action. On June 25, 1913, the General Assembly of the Commonwealth of Pennsylvania passed Act #555 regulating the construction of dams in the state.

Remains of the dam
© Patt Historical Society

Remains of the town © Patt Historical Society

As for the tall man in black, well he was never seen again. Was he a harbinger warning of danger to come? Was he there to warn the town about the dam? Could all this have been prevented had someone asked him? Although this occurred years earlier, some believe it was similar to the sightings of the Mothman near Point Pleasant, West Virginia, who appeared before the collapse of the Silver Bridge across the Ohio River on December 15, 1967.

Collapse of the Silver Bridge – December 15, 1967
©The Herald Dispatch West Virginia

Chapter 6
Lake Michigan Triangle

Lake Michigan is part of the massive North American body of waters known as the Great Lakes. The system includes Lakes Erie, Huron, Michigan, Ontario, and Superior which in total contain 84% of the fresh water in North America. Lake Superior is the second largest lake in the world by area and the largest fresh water lake by area. At 307 miles long and 118 miles wide, Lake Michigan is the second largest of the lakes by volume, and the third largest by surface area. It is the only Great Lake completely within the United States boundaries. It averages 279 feet deep and has 1640 miles of shoreline on which 12 million people call home. With its many beaches it is referred to as the third Coast of the United States after those of the Atlantic Ocean and the Pacific Ocean. In addition, there are over 111,000 acres of sand dunes lining the shores making it the largest fresh water dune system in the world.

The conditions leading up to the formation of the Great Lakes began one billion years ago when two tectonic plates, the earth's two upper most layers consisting of the crust and mantle, split apart forming the Midcontinent Rift that is 1200 miles long. Because of this a valley was formed that provided a basin that would become Lake Superior. With the second fault line, the Saint Lawrence Rift which split approximately 570 million years ago, Lake Erie and Lake Ontario were created along with the St. Lawrence River. Finally at the end of the last glacial period, the Wisconsin Glaciations that ended 10,000-12,000 years ago when the Lawrence Ice Sheet receded, the retreat of the ice left a huge amount of melt water that filled up the basins that the glaciers had previously carved, thus creating Lakes Michigan and Huron.

The name of each of the lakes is derived from Native words. Erie: the Iroquoian word "eriehonan" or "long tail;" Huron: the Wyandat or Huron Nation word "karegnondi" meaning "lake of the Hurons;" Michigan: the Ojibwe word "mishiogami" or "great water;" Ontario: the Wyandat word "ontari io" meaning "lake of shining waters;" and Superior: the Ojibwe word "gichi gami" or "big water."

The earliest inhabitants of the region were the Hopewell culture that lived there during the Woodland Period from 100 B.C. to 400 A.D. Based on artifacts found there including items made with copper, iron, and silver, it is believed that they had a high level of intelligence and traded with the Aztecs and Mayans of Mexico. When the Ottawa people migrated from Canada to Michigan they spoke of this culture as the Yam-Ko-Desh or "prairie people." They avoided the burial mounds of the Hopewell saying their spirits still roam there. Today eleven burial mounds known as the Norton Mounds remain in a forest outside of Grand Rapids. They were named after Captain A.N. Norton who owned the land in the 1800's.

Three largest mounds along the Grand River

By the 12 century, the area was inhabited by the Ojibwe, Odawa, Potowatami, Mascouten, and Miami people. In 1620, French born Etienne Brule an interpreter and guide was the first to explore the Great Lakes region.

While many people admired the beauty of these waters, to some they took on an ominous reputation. Lake Michigan's tales began to be as mysterious as the water itself.

Old time sailors remarked that she bears a weight that is a burden to carry and even refused to cross her unforgiving waters. Today these great waters are referred to as the Lake Michigan Triangle. The coordinates of the Lake Michigan Triangle extend from Ludington, Michigan to Benton Harbor, Michigan over to Manitowoc, Wisconsin and back to Ludington. Just like the infamous Bermuda Triangle, there are claims of ghost ships, disappearing planes and crew members, strange weather phenomenon and tales of big green sea monsters. Some even attest to the fact that it is a vortex that slows or speeds up time.

Lake Michigan Triangle

El Griffin

French explorer Rene-Robert Cavelier de La Salle arrived in America in 1666. He had been granted permission by King Louis XVI to explore the New World in order to search for a Northwest Passageway to China. During his quest he claimed much of the Great Lakes region and the Mississippi River basin for King Louis XVI of France. He built a ship called le Griffon, a forty-five ton barque with three masts, forty feet long, and seven canons in order to explore the Great Lakes region in the late 17th century. It was the first European ship to sail the upper Great Lakes and the first to vanish in Lake Michigan.

On August 7, 1679, La Salle and his partner Father Louis Hennepin set out on their maiden voyage with a crew of thirty-two men. They sailed across Lakes Erie, Huron, and Michigan through uncharted waters that had previously only been explored by canoes where they conducted fur trading. On September 12, La Salle, Hennepin, and most of the crew set out in canoes to connect with some other fur traders in La Grand Baie, which is now known as Green Bay. The Griffon with Luke the Dane, so called because he was seven feet tall, and five other crew members was ordered to sail back to

Mackinac Island with a load of furs totaling $12,000. However, their journey was hindered as a huge storm passed through. They waited out the storm that lasted four days and on September 16 when it appeared that the storm had passed, they set out on their voyage. The ship was never seen again.

El Griffin

St.Alban

January 30, 1881, the St. Albans steamer, carrying a cargo of flour and livestock, was forced to abandon ship as it began to sink near Milwaukee, Wisconsin. The twenty men and six passengers managed to swim safely to shore as the ship slowly succumbed to the abyss. Then in late February, fishermen along the Fox Islands began seeing the same ghostly steam boat with smoke coming from its stacks floating without a crew.

St. Albans Steamer

The Mary McLane
The Fury of Cloudless Sky

July 12, 1883, the Mary McLane tugboat was just off the Chicago Harbor. Suddenly, at 6:00 p.m. they were hit with a barrage of large chunks of ice the size of bricks that had begun falling out of the cloudless sky. The ice was large enough to put dents in the wooden deck. The crew was baffled and ran for cover while it continued for thirty minutes. One of the crew members took some blocks home and found they weighed about two pounds.

The Tomas Hume

The Thomas Hume schooner was built in Manitowoc, Wisconsin, in 1870. The ship was christened as H.C. Albrecht in honor of its first owner Captain Harry Albrecht. In 1976, the ship was sold to Captain Welch from Chicago. The following year, the ship was bought by Charles Hockley, a lumber baron who owned the Hackley-Hume Lumber Mill on Muskegon Lake. The Hume would make several successful trips across Lake Michigan until May 21, 1891. The schooner with Captain George C. Albrecht was sailing from Chicago, Illinois to Muskegon, Michigan after just having dropped off a load of lumber, but it never completed its voyage. It disappeared without a trace taking with it the captain and seven sailors. It was found 115 years later in 2006 when the A&T Recovery Diving team found it in the southeastern part of the lake still in remarkably good condition.

The Rosa Belle

House of David

October of 1921, the schooner Rosa Belle steered by Captain Erhardt Geise was carrying eleven members of the Benton Harbor House of David. The House of David began in 1903 with Benjamin Purnell who claimed to be a Prophet, the Seventh and final Messenger of God. It was a live-in commune, though some called it a cult, which promised eternal life to those who joined him and obeyed him. Unfortunately, for reasons unknown they never reached their destination. On October 30, the Grand Trunk car ferry Ann Arbor #4 discovered the wreckage floating upside down. Yet there was no trace of the passengers. The aft section was smashed, the cabin was wrenched away from the deck and the ship's rigging was floating loosely above the hull. Coincidentally, forty-six years earlier, the Rosa Belle was in her first wreck. She floated almost directly across from the location where she met her final end in 1921.

The Rosa Belle

Wreckage of the Rosa Belle
© Sheboygan Press-Telegraph

The O.M. McFarland
Disappearance of Captain George Donner

In August 1875, the freighter O.M. McFarland mysteriously capsized in Lake Michigan. All ten crew members were lost and their bodies were never found. She later drifted ashore near Grand Haven, Michigan where the wreckage was recovered and rebuilt.

April 28, 1937, the O.M. McFarland with Captain George Donner was in route to Port Washington, Wisconsin. The Captain decided to retire to his cabin after the vessel had cleared the ice-choked Straits of Maschinaw and turned south through Lake Michigan toward Port Washington. He asked to be awakened when they had reached shore. When the second mate went to wake him at 6:00 p.m., there was no answer. He found the door was secured from the inside, and concerned that something was amiss, he broke down the door only to discover the cabin empty. They searched the entire ship, but Captain Donner had disappeared and was never found.

Three Sisters

Legends abound as to what malevolent forces may have contributed to the demise of many ships. Sailors have spoken of the "Three Sisters" phenomenon that lures unsuspecting vessels into their clutches only to viciously lash out at them. During bad storms, giant waves sometimes as high as ten feet tall travel in groups of three with a calm pause in between. Legend has it that even though many ships after surviving the first two waves succumbed to the third becoming just another victim to the Three Sisters.

Three Sisters

Death's Door

Porte de Morts the French word meaning "Death's Door" is a straight of water between the tip of the Wisconsin Door Peninsula and Washington Island containing the Potawatomi Islands that links Lake Michigan and Green Bay. Natives and sailors both believe the waterway to be haunted. Here one might hear the panicked cries of drowning men or see ghost ships.

In the 1700's, the Potawatomi set out from the islands in order to attack the Winnebago on the mainland. Likewise, the Winnebago headed out into the waterway to confront their rivals. What began as a calm day suddenly turned deadly as the treacherous waves trapped their canoes tossing them against the rocky shores killing hundreds. It is said their spirits still haunt the waters. Death's Door feared because of its unpredictable waves, rapids and whirlpools, is responsible for more shipwrecks than any other section of fresh water in the world.

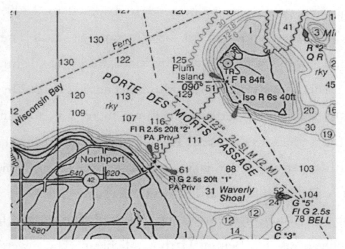

Porte de Morts – Death's Door

Disappearance of Northwest Flight 2501

The waters of the Michigan Triangle are not its only mysterious element. Look up to the sky where numerous unexplainable phenomena abound. To date, almost forty planes have vanished. One such incident was on June 23, 1950, as Northwest Airlines Flight 2501 a DC-4 took off from New York City heading to Minneapolis, Minnesota carrying a crew of three and fifty-five passengers. Captain Robert C. Lind served the pilot and Verne F. Wolfe was First Officer.

At 11:37 a.m. near Chicago, Illinois, the pilot

requested permission to descend from 3,500 to 2,500 feet
because they appeared to be entering a squall line of
thunderstorms with high velocity winds, heavy rain, lightning,
and hail. However, permission to descend was denied by the
Civil Aeronautic Authority because there was too much
traffic at the lower altitude. The pilot proceeded to head in a
northwesterly direction taking the plane over Lake Michigan.
The estimated time of arrival over Milwaukee was 11:51 a.m.
The plane suddenly went off the radar and plunged into Lake
Michigan just off Benton Harbor, Michigan. There were no
survivors. Just minutes before, witnesses reported hearing
engine sputtering sounds and a strange red light appeared in
the sky in Wisconsin disappearing after ten minutes.

Very little traces of the plane were found. The aircraft
log book was discovered floating in the water. The only clue
as to what might have occurred was a plywood oxygen bottle
support bracket. The bracket had been installed on the
forward left side of the fuselage which meant the impact
force that had ripped it off must have been forward,
downward, and to the left. It was also speculated by the
Douglas Aircraft Company that perhaps the aircraft had
turned on its back.

Detroit Free Press - June 24, 1950

Somewhere in the Skies

At 4:00 a.m. on March 14, 1966, Deputies Bushroe and Foster observed a line of four objects with red and green flashing lights in the sky. They watched for an hour as the objects moved at a great speed doing maneuvers that a plane was not capable of doing. They would shoot upward at a tremendous speed, hover, and then come back down just as fast. In addition, they reported seeing four identical objects at 4:20 and two additional ones at 4:54. Police began receiving calls from numerous people reporting seeing strange high speed lights in the sky. Selfridge Air National Guard Base in Mount Clemens, Michigan confirmed observing strange anomalies during the same time period.

On March 17 at 4:25 a.m. Sargent Nuel Schneider and

Deputy David Fitzpatrick viewed a top-shaped craft in the sky. They watched as the lights dimmed, brightened, and slowly disappeared. At 10:32 a.m. the same day, seventeen college students observed a strange craft with red, orange, and white lights that came from the northeast and disappeared to the south.

On March 20, Frank Nannor was walking his dog before dinner when he observed a domed oval object with lights in the center up in the sky. After dinner, he heard the dog barking outside and he and his son Ron went out to investigate. They saw a strange light above them and it began to descend. But instead of landing, it remained motionless hovering over the treetops in the woods near the swampland.

He notified the police and Deputies Stanley McFadden and David Fitzpatrick came out to investigate. Before they arrived Frank and his son walked closer when suddenly a strange craft about the size of an automobile appeared out of nowhere right in front of them. The entire area lit up as if somebody had shown a giant spotlight on them. A strange mist emerged from the bottom of the craft changing in color from green, red, to white. Then it vanished, only to reappear a few moments later except in a different spot. This happened several more times before the object suddenly ascended straight upward and flew into the sky right over the Deputies that had just arrived.

Because of all the sightings reported by numerous people, police, and the Air National Guard Base, Michigan Congressman Weston Vivian requested that the U.S. Air Force should dispatch an investigator from Project Blue Book to assess the situation.

Dr. Josef Allen Hynek from Northwestern was assigned the task. Dr. Hynek proceeded to the Nannor property and spent a total of two hours and forty-five minutes before concluding his investigation.

He drove to the county sheriff station where he met with Sheriff Douglas Harvey. Engaging in conversation with the sheriff, he told him that he concluded there was something very strange by the farm and it definitely warranted further investigation. Before he could get too in depth into his findings, he received a phone call that lasted quite a long time. When he returned, his demeanor was different and he changed his story informing the sheriff that the many sightings were merely the moon and stars.

What the men had actually seen at the farm was a natural occurring phenomena called "swamp gas." On March 25, he told reporters at a press conference the identical story. Why did he suddenly change his findings? Was it a government cover-up?

Dr. J. Allen Hynek and Dexter Police Chief Robert Taylor looking over the map of UFO sightings

Detroit Free Press – March 22, 1966

Detroit Free Press – March 22, 1966

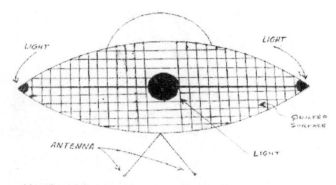

After the sightings, the witnesses put together this composite drawing at the Washtenaw County sheriff's headquarters, showing the lights, surface and antenna.

Witness Drawing of Craft

Dr. Josef Allen Hynek
Michigan press conference

Not satisfied with the findings of the investigation, Congressman Gerald Ford called for a congressional investigation on March 28, 1966. He remarked, "In the firm belief that the American public deserves a better explanation than that thus far given by the Air Force, I strongly recommend there be a committee investigation of the UFO phenomena. I think we owe it to the people to establish credibility regarding UFOs and produce the greatest possible enlightenment of the subject."

Congressman Gerald Ford

March 28, 1966

Rep. George P. Miller, Chairman   Rep. L. Mendel Rivers, Chairman
Science and Astronautics Committee   Armed Services Committee
U. S. House of Representatives   U. S. House of Representatives
Washington, D.C.   Washington, D. C.

Dear Chairmen Miller and Rivers:

No doubt you have noted the recent flurry of newspaper stories about
unidentified flying objects (UFO's). I have taken special interest in
these accounts because many of the latest reported sightings have been
in my home state of Michigan.

The Air Force sent a consultant, astrophysicist Dr. J. Allen Hynek of
Northwestern University, to Michigan to investigate the various reports;
and he dismissed all of them as the product of college student pranks or
swamp gas or an impression created by the rising crescent moon and the
planet Venus. I do not agree that all of these reports can be or should
be so easily explained away.

Because I think there may be substance to some of these reports and
because I believe the American people are entitled to a more thorough
explanation than has been given them by the Air Force to date, I am
proposing that either the Science and Astronautics Committee or the
Armed Services Committee of the House schedule hearings on the subject
of UFO's and invite testimony from both the executive branch of the
government and some of the persons who claim to have seen UFO's.

I enclose material which I think will be helpful to you in assessing the
advisability of an investigation of UFO's.

May I first call to your attention a column by Roscoe Drummond, published
last Sunday in which Mr. Drummond says, "Maybe all of these reported
sightings are whimsical, imaginary or unreal; but we need a more credible
and detached appraisal of the evidence than we are getting."

Mr. Drummond goes on to state, "We need to get all the data drawn together
to one place and examined far more objectively than anyone has done so far.
A stable public opinion will come from a trustworthy look at the evidence,
not from belittling it."

"The time has come for the President or Congress to name an objective and
respected panel to investigate, appraise, and report on all present and
future evidence about what is going on."

I agree fully with Mr. Drummond's statements. I also suggest you scan
the enclosed series of six articles by Bulkley Griffin of the Griffin-
Larrabee News Bureau here. In the last of his articles, published last
January, Mr. Griffin says, "A main conclusion can be briefly stated. It
is that the Air Force is misleading the public by its continuing campaign
to produce and maintain belief that all sightings can be explained away
as misidentification of familiar objects, such as balloons, stars, and
aircraft."

I have just today received a number of telegrams urging a congressional
investigation of UFO's. One is from retired Air Force Col. Harold R. Brown,
Ardmore, Tennessee, who says, "I have seen UFO. Will be available to
testify."

Another, from Mrs. Ethyle M. Davis, Eugene, Oregon, reads, "Nine out of
ten people want truth of UFO's Press your investigation to the fullest."

Congressman Gerald Ford's letter to Representative George P.
Miller, Science and Astronautics Committee and Representative L.
Mendel Rivers, Armed Service Committee – March 28, 1966

Dale Goudie, Director of Pudget Sound Aerial Phenomena Research and Information for the UFO Information Service in Seattle, Washington shared the findings of a scientific analysis of the soil, water, and animal life from the landing site. It was revealed the soil had a slightly above normal content of radiation and high amount of boron which is found in meteoroids. Microscopic organisms in the water were dead. Amphibians appeared sluggish although no metabolic changes could be detected. Normally green plants and fungi were now yellow. Blue pigments did not show up in the test and were presumed destroyed.

Laboratory Analysis Results of 1966 Swampgas Case

This information was obtained by Mr. Dale Goudie, Director of Puget Sound Aerial Phenomena Research and Information Director for the UFO Reporting and Information Service in Seattle, Washington.

The broad details of this case have long been known. This is the case in which Dr. J. Allen Hynek, at the time a consultant to the U.S. Air Force, issued his quickly condemned opinion that the lights seen could have been swamp gas.

New additional information about the famed 1966 Swamp Gas case in Michigan surfaced in 1986 shedding new light on this incident.

The material consists of a news release issued at the time by William E. Van Horn, the Civil Defense Director for Hillsdale County, Michigan. It contains a hitherto unknown laboratory report covering the scientific analysis of soil, water and animal life in the area of the reported landing. For those unfamiliar with the case, here are excerpts from a statement made at the time by Mr. Van Horn:

On the evening of March 21,1966 at 10:42 p.m., a call was received from the New Women's Dormitory at Hillsdale College by the Office Of Civil Defense... from a student reporting that some type of craft had descended from the Northeast, flashed by their dormitory and disappeared to the South. At this time, the girl described as well as later, the observing of red, green and white pulsating lights. There were 17 of the college students that made this observation.

At approximately 11 p.m., a second call was made by the girl to the Civil Defense Office informing them that the object had reappeared and had settled close to the ground approximately one half mile from the dormitory. Van Horn at once called for help from the Police Department and three cars plus himself were sent in a two mile area from the dormitory to the East. Van Horn checked the area at the half mile point and after he was unable to locate anything. He at once returned to the dormitory.

Upon arriving at the dormitory, he was escorted to the second floor and taken to a room facing the east, from where he made the following observation. He observed that there was an object which was at an approximate distance of 1,500 to 1,700 feet away from them... settled into a hollow and was apparently either near or on the ground. The two lights upon his first observation were what he would describe as a dim orange on the right and a dirty white on the left. After observing this for a period of about 10 minutes the lights began to grow in brilliance, the dim orange became red and true in color and the white became a true white. As the lights became more brilliant, the object or vehicle began to rise.

It would rise to a height of approximately 100 to 150 feet, stop momentarily and begin to descend. This occurred several times. At one time upon descending, a glow from the side opposite them came from somewhere and he was able to see a contoured surface.

The vehicle was also observed to move right to left, and left to right, and did so in a very smooth manner. The ascent and descent were at an estimated rate of 25 to 30 feet per minute. [This was estimated from Van Horns experience as a commercial pilot.] At no time were any of the witnesses able to detect any type of sound or noise.

At approximately 4:30 a.m., those still observing the scene noticed the lights disappear and this was the last that was seen of it.

The area that this was observed in was by no means a swamp but rather an area which is cultivated by Hillsdale College as a park.

Goudie also states that there will be additional information up coming and will be released in a short time by the UFO Reporting and Information Service in Seattle. This new information will even bring us closer to the reality of this case and keep this in mind that this case was investigated very carefully.

Lab Results Of 1966 Swamp Gas Case

page 2

1. SOIL TESTS

a. Acid-Base Test

Acid content of three, which is very heavy, and Base content of seven or eight, which is almost neutral.

b. Solubility Test

The soil was very soluble in a water solution.

c. Composition Test

There was no change in soil composition except for a slight additive of Boron.

d. Radiological Test

The radiation reading on the soil was thirtyone hundredths roentgens per hour. (.31 r/hr)

2. PLANT TESTS

(Green and Fungi)

a. Paper Chromatography Test

There were found only green and yellow pigments in this test; the blue pigment did not show up in this test, so we presume the blue pigment was destroyed.

b. Tests for Measuring Life Functions

The plants were found to be healthy.

c. Starch Test

This was found to be normal.

d. Chlorophyll Test

This was found to be normal.

e. Radiological Test

The reading on the plants was three/hundred fifteen thousandths roentgens per hour. (.315 r/hr)

f. Spectrum Test On Plant Chlorophyll

The blue pigment was gone; it did not show up in this test, presuming again that the blue pigment was completely destroyed.

CUFON - Computer UFO Network Analysis Report
Dale Gordie Information Director

CONCLUSIONS

1. SOIL:
The soil had above normal radiation and also had abnormal content of Boron.

2. PLANT:
The plants had above normal radiation. Blue pigments did not show up in the tests and were presumed to be destroyed, but this did not seem to effect the life junctions of the plants.

3. POND LIFE:
Crustation and Amphibian radiation was higher than normal but the highest radiation was recorded in the Amphibian. Also the Amphibian was affected noiceably where the Crustation was not.

4. MINERAL:
Sedimentary rocks were slightly higher in radiation than either ingenous or metamorphic rocks. There was no other change either chemical or structural.

5. WATER:
All microscopic plants animals were dead. The water had above normal radiation and abnormally contained Boron.

6. ENVIRONMENT:
The environment had above normal radiation and it contained a small amount of Boron which is foreign to this soil.

7. MAIN CONCLUSION:
The area contained an abnormally high amount of radiation from some unknown source. The area also strangely contained Boron which was found in both water and soil. These two facts are the only ones which would substantiate the presence of a U.F.O. In our opinion, we're not saying that there was a U.F.O., but we also do not know how to arcunt for these two facts. However, we believe it could not be swamp gas because of the high winds on the night of the sighting. With these high winds the gas would not have formed a mass and remained stationary. We also do not believe it was pranksters because we searched the area thoroughly for any sign of evidence to explain the phenomenon.

NOTE: Radioactive decay took place at 9.6 milliroentgens per hour over a period of three hours.

C U F O N

Computer UFO Network

Seattle Washington, USA

(206) 776-0382 # Data Bits, No Parity, 1 Stop Bit 300/1200/2400 bps.

SYSOP - Jim Klotz Information Director - Dale Goodie

UFO Reporting and Information Service
Voice Line - unavailableP.O.Mail unavailable, Mercer Island, WA 98040, USA

- Please credit CUFON as the source of this material -

CUFON - Computer UFO Network Analysis Report
Dale Gordie Information Director

Swamp Gas ... what exactly is it? A swamp is a place of rotting vegetation and decomposion. Gases are produced from the microbial breakdown of the vegetation in the absence of oxygen. These gases are a mixture of carbon dioxide, methane, and hydrogen sulfide. The gases ignite tiny flames or lights that are sometimes seen on the ground or appear to be rising and floating above it. The flames, yellow, red, or blue green, may go out in one place and then suddenly appear in another giving off the illusion of motion. There is no actual heat radiating from the lights and they do not burn the ground. The lights may appear for hours or continue throughout the night.

Swamp Gas

Ufologists maintain that the findings of the testing substantiate the presence of extra-terrestrials and the event was not the result of Swamp Gas. In fact, because of the high winds that evening, it would not be plausible to suggest that the gases could have formed a mass and remained in one position for any length of time. By April of 1966, all research of the event had ceased, but the name Swamp Gas will always remain synonymous with Michigan.

The Ludington Lights

On March 8, 1994, around 9:30 p.m. eerie lights were observed in the sky along nearly 200 miles of the Lake Michigan shoreline extending from Ludington, Michigan, south to the Indiana border. The 991 Operators were being flooded with calls as reports from over 300 people including police and meteorologists came through. One operator contacted the National Weather Service radar operator in Muskegon. Meteorologist Leo Grwenier stated that he recorded three unknown echoes on his radar at the time in question that appeared for about fifteen minutes. At times they were moving at 5 to 12,000 feet in the air before they drifted slowly in a south, southwest direction and headed toward the Chicago side of the southern end of Lake Michigan. He knew the objects were not planes because planes show up as pinpoints on the scope. These were much larger at about half the size of his thumb nail.

Holland Police Officer Jeff Velthouse also observed the strange lights noting there were five to six objects, some of them cylindrical in shape with red, blue, white, and green lights that were sometimes performing unusual maneuvers. The mystery of one of the largest UFO mass sightings in Michigan history since 1966 remains unsolved to this day.

Ann Arbor News Bureau - March 9, 1994

Detroit Free Press – March 9, 1994

The Paulding Light

On June 13, 2016, a group of teens reported to the sheriff that they had observed a strange light in a valley just outside of Paulding, Michigan near Old US 45. It is said the light rises over the horizon, sometimes changes color, and varies in intensity as it appears to move up and down or side to side before disappearing. Locals contend that the Paulding Light appears almost every night.

Legend has it that railroad tracks once ran through the valley. The light is the lantern belonging to the brakeman

181

who was killed as he attempted to stop an oncoming train from colliding with railway cars which were stopped on the tracks.

Paulding Light

The Manitowoc Incident

The Point Beach Nuclear Plant is located on approximately 1,200 acres near the city of Two Creeks, Wisconsin, in Manitowoc County. The power generated from this plant services the Green Bay area and communities along the Lake Michigan shoreline of southwest Wisconsin.

On March 24, 2019, about 8:30 p.m. U.S. Marine Corp veteran Myles Panosh was talking on the phone with his friend Shelly Schmidt of Sheboygan, Wisconsin. They were discussing UFO experiences.

He was sitting near a window upstairs when suddenly he looked out and observed a huge light hovering over the vicinity of the Point Beach Nuclear Plant in nearby Two Creeks. Being a trained military observer, he was certain it was not a star, planet, or meteor. It was not a lighthouse or city lights. He remarked to Shelly that he and some residents had previously observed some strange lights in the sky, but nothing like this had ever been reported. It did not look like any military craft that we currently have. It was definitely an Unidentified Flying Object.

He attempted to capture the image with his iPhone, but the resolution was not very good. Not wanting to miss an opportunity to film this event, at 8:45 p.m. he decided to contact his friend Jeff Lavicka who was a videographer and who also lived two miles to the north-east closer to the lake. Jeff was immediately able to successfully film fifteen minutes of the mysterious incident.

The two men watched as a hug reddish-orange glowing light hovered over the nuclear plant. Multi-colored lights appeared at the apexes of a wedge-shaped craft. It was accompanied on and off by other smaller luminous bodies, red, orange, green, blue, and yellow, that began to cascade around the large light. They were twinkling like a Christmas tree. Sometimes a "line" of light would drop from one light to another and they would flash. They couldn't be certain whether these small lights were approaching or emerging from the huge one. There were no stars or other celestial bodies that were visible in the night sky. This suggested that the object's luminous emissions were brighter than starlight and were operating within Earth's atmosphere. They continued to watch the event that was visible until 11:30 p.m.

Although some employees at the plant at times observed strange lights in the night sky above them, it was not a topic they spoke of publicly. There had been some instances of groundwater leaks at the facility. They did not want to draw attention to such things as extra-terrestrial activity. If the security system sensors at the plant ever indicated any unknown objects in the air, nobody ever revealed such information to the public. There are some ufologists that believe UFOs over nuclear plants are actually benevolent beings watching over us.

Point Beach Nuclear Facility – Two Creeks, WI

Myles Panosh

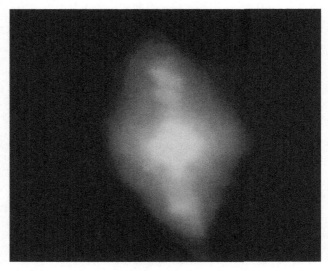

Bright Light over Point Beach Nuclear Plant
March 24, 2019

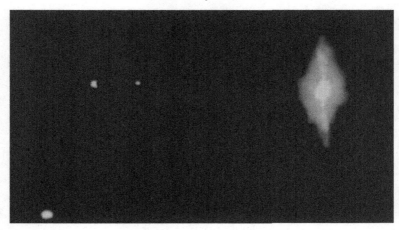

Meteor Impact

In the evening of November 26, 2019, people in South East Michigan, Northern Indiana, North Eastern, Illinois, and the South East corner of Wisconsin witnessed a brilliant light in the sky over southern Lake Michigan. Reports of two large balls of fire fell from the sky into the lake, exploding on impact. This was followed by a deep and prolonged rumbling and shaking of the earth.

O'Hare International Airport UFOs

On May 22, 2000, O'Hare International Airport in Chicago, Illinois began observing strange images of thirteen "ghost planes" on their radar in the skies over the triangle. Worried that planes might succumb to a mid-air collision, several flights were instructed to change their course. There were so many sightings of unidentified flying objects and phantom planes surrounding that time period that it prompted the Federal Aviation Administration to create a top secret Lake Report file to catalog their findings.

187

At 1:25 a.m. on February 2, 2017, over 200 reports streamed in from Michigan, Wisconsin, and Illinois as a meteor was sighted in the night sky. The blue-green fireball was traveling from southwest to northeast before it hit somewhere near Lake Michigan between Sheboygan and Manitowoc, Wisconsin. The boom heard in Michigan was not a crash, but actually a sonic boom as it traveled more than forty times the speed of sound. It was estimated the meteor, considered a "super bolide," was two yards in diameter. A super bolide is a fireball with a magnitude of -14 or brighter which is more than twice as bright as the moon.

The Serpent

The Michigan Triangle also contains an abundance of mysterious cryptids. The Ojibwe spoke about a great serpent in the lake that possessed mystical powers. Many early sailors also claimed to have encountered the creature. In 1867, a fisherman named Joseph Muklke reported seeing a huge serpent within twenty feet of his boat. It was swimming about a mile and a half off the shoreline of the south side of Chicago. The scaled serpent was fifty feet long, very dark blue with a grayish belly. In 1934, Captain G.E. Stufflebeam of the U.S.S. Theodore Roosevelt and his crew spotted the serpent about four miles off shore. Others claimed to hear it making roaring sounds in the distance much like a bull. Chicago newspapers had the city in an uproar when they reported the sightings from 1867-1890.

The Dogman

They also spoke of a mysterious entity known as the Dogman. The creature 6-7 feet tall with yellow eyes is half man and half dog with the ability to walk on two legs. Elders claim the Dogman was a member of a shape shifting tribe that is stuck somewhere between their human and animal form. The first documented sighting was in 1887 when two lumberjacks in Wexford County spotted the creature. Most modern day encounters are primarily in Wisconsin and the Lower Peninsula of Michigan. Many reports center around ancient effigy mounds such as those in Wisconsin and Traverse City, Michigan. Wisconsin is the site of the largest number of effigy mounds in the United States. It is estimated they were built during the Late Woodland Period around 1400-750 A.D. An effigy is a raised pile of earth built in the shape of an animal. It is believed these earthworks were built to mark celestial events and seasonal observations. Did the builders also leave behind guardians such as the Dogman to protect the sacred mounds?

189

Michigan Dogman

Sasquatch

Michigan comprised of many forests, makes it the perfect environment for Sasquatch. In fact, with 1131 documented cases from present day back to the War of 1812, the state ranks 4th following Washington, California, and Pennsylvania. The word Sasquatch is derived from "sasq'ets" meaning "wild man." Native elders revered the creature saying it was a forest spirit and called it brother.

The earliest recorded sighting was in 1878. It happened when a woman was in the yard hanging the wash and she heard a strange noise. She glanced up to see a huge hairy man-like creature looking at her. Frightened, she ran to the saw mill to tell her husband. However, when they returned, the creature was nowhere to be found. The only indication it had been there were some very huge footprints.

Hunters began encountering more wildlife than they had anticipated. In 1917, two hunters had just brought down a deer. Suddenly, a huge hairy man emerged from the bushes, picked up the carcass, and walked away with it tucked under his arm.

One hot spot for Bigfoot is the Huron National Forest named after the Huron Nation which is located in the Lower Peninsula of Michigan. It measures 437,287 acres extending seventy miles east to west and thirty miles north to south. On the south lies the Muskegon River and towards the north are several swamps including the Foley Swamp. The latest sighting in 2019, occurred as two people driving down the winding road, witnessed a seven foot tall dark hairy creature standing in the middle of the road. Suddenly, it turned and ran off covering a distance from the road and up the hill in eight steps.

American Stonehenge

In 2007, Mark Holley a professor of underwater archeology at Northwestern Michigan University and fellow colleague Brian Abbot were voyaging across the lake in a ship containing sonar equipment in pursuit of locating old ship wrecks. Along with their many findings, they were astonished upon discovering a circular formation of prehistoric rocks forty feet below the water where the Grand Traverse Bay Underwater Preserve is located. These appeared to be from an ancient civilization with the grouping being characteristic to the iconic Stonehenge of the UK.

Nicknamed the American Stonehenge, it consists of a circle of tall vertical stones and some petroglyph sites. One huge boulder standing outside of the circle measuring four feet high and five feet long contains a drawing that represents a mastodon which has been extinct for over 10,000 years.

According to geographical history, around 10,500 years ago, the water level had dropped and drained to a much lower level for about 3,500 years. It would have been possible to inhabit the land and have a water supply nearby. It is likely that the stone circle was constructed during the last Ice Age about 6000-9000 years ago when the lake bed would have been tundra. Then 5000 years ago, at the end of the Ice Age the water level rose and the basin filled again.

Dr. John O'Shea is the Curator of Great Lakes Archaeology at the University of Michigan Museum of Anthropological Archaeology. He contends that the formation was a hunting structure known as a "drive lane' that ancient hunters used. Drive lanes were used as a means to herd large groups of animals along a certain path to a "kill zone" where hunters were waiting. Possible inhabitants were the Hopewell or Late Woodland.

Underwater "Stonehenge"
© Mark Holley and Brian Abbot

Petroglyph of a Mastodon

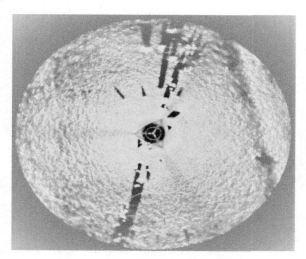

View of entire formation
© Mark Holley and Brian Abbot

Chapter 7
Little Egypt Triangle

The southern tip of Illinois forms an area known as the "Little Egypt Triangle." The region is bordered by the most voluminous rivers in the United States. The Wabash and Ohio Rivers are to the east and south, and the Mississippi River and its connecting Missouri River is to the west.

Little Egypt Triangle

Although there is not actually any documented correlation with the land near the Nile, there is one story that is often shared. In 1799, Minister John Badgley was riding a horse high on top the bluff overlooking a wide plane that stretched from what is now Alton to Chester. What he saw that day reminded him of the story in the bible where the Israelites fled to Egypt and the fertile Nile Valley. The geographic features of the Nile Valley described in the bible were strikingly similar to the Mississippi River Valley, the many mounds with their pyramid like characteristics and the air of mystery in what might lie beyond. Perhaps this was his intention when he named the area the "Land of Goshen," an Egyptian word meaning "best of the land." Years later the settlement of Goshen changed its name to Edwardsville.

The area's ties with Egypt are eerily evident as with the reference to cities such as Memphis, Thebes, Karnak, Cairo, and Dongola. One might contemplate why each name was chosen. Was there a correlation with these cities along the Mississippi River to those along the Nile? Could there have been a special significance about the Egyptian origin?

According to Egyptian mythology, Memphis on the west bank of the Nile was the home of Ptak the deity who existed before all things and by his will thought the world into existence. Thebes on the east bank was the first city founded on a sacred mound which was believed to have risen from the waters of chaos at the beginning of time. It was upon this mound that Amon the god of sun and air stood and would be the breath of life which created all souls. Karnak on the east bank was known as the "Throne of Two

Lands." It was the ancient site of the Temple of Amun and ancient observatory where Ptak would communicate with the people of Earth. Cairo located on the Nile Delta obtained its name "The Conqueror" because the planet Mars was rising at the same time the city was founded.

In 1673, the French were the first European settlers to arrive in the northern part of Illinois later migrating south traveling by way of the Ohio River. They named the area Illinois after the Illiniwek people that welcomed them there. Here they operated a fur trading post along the Mississippi River.

It was the French who introduced slavery to Illinois. In 1719, Philip Frances Renault brought 500 slaves from San Domingo hoping to develop a mine. When the venture proved unsuccessful, he sold them to plantation owners and returned to France. For many years plantations used a proportionately amount of slaves to toil in the cotton and tobacco fields. Slavery would continue in Illinois even after it was prohibited in 1787 under the Northwest Ordinance because the plantation owners felt the crops could only be grown profitably with slave labor. Many were forced to sign indentures of 40-99 years and were threatened to be sold if they refused. An indentured servant worked for the land owner for a specific time and then would be granted freedom.

Others who were emancipated lived very restricted lives constantly fearing the unjust repercussions of the Black Code. These laws allowed local authorities to arrest any freemen for minor infractions where as they would become part of the convict lease system. Through this system the authorities would provide prison labor to private entities such as plantation owners. Some described this as slavery by another name.

Yet, Illinois also served as a proverbial path to freedom for those who dreamed of a better life. Here they sought out the Underground Railroad that operated actively in Southern Illinois. The Underground Railroad was a multitude of secret routes with safe houses called stations owned by people known as conductors that afforded fugitive slaves and freemen the opportunity to complete self-emancipation. Illinois bordered two slave states Missouri and Kentucky. The Illinois River played a key role because slaves had to cross the Mississippi River to enter the Illinois River. It was at the convergence of these two rivers that the Underground Railroad began.

The Railroad consisted of two "liberty" lines. One point began in Cairo where today there are still tunnels beneath the town once used by travelers. The second point was in Chester. The two lines merged at Centralia and extended all the way north to Chicago. A third line began in Alton going up the Illinois River into Chicago. Once they had reached this destination, they boarded a boat to freedom in Canada. Directions to railroad travelers were coded in Bible verses or songs and the story of Moses' fleeing Egypt was used as an analog. Here again is another reference to Egypt. It is estimated that almost 100,000 people escaped to their freedom.

The earliest inhabitants of Illinois are thought to have arrived around 12,000 B.C. They were known as the Clovis people from Siberia who were nomadic hunter-gatherers. It is speculated that they migrated to North America coming across the Bering Strait. The Woodland culture occupied the land from 600-900 A.D. followed by the Mississippian in 900A.D.

Cahokia, located within the boundaries of present day Collinsville was the largest and most influenced settlements in the Mississippian culture. At one time its peak population was between 25,000 and 50, 000 people. It was comprised of three boroughs Cahokia, East St. Louis, and St. Louis connected to each other by waterways and walking trails that extended across the Mississippi River flood plane for eight miles.

Carbon dating has placed the beginning of the site to 1000-1050 A.D. Archeologists believe the construction of Cahokia was related to a supernova SN1006 that occurred between April 30 and May 1 in 1006 A.D. in the constellation Lupus of the Milky Way. It was estimated to have been the brightest stellar event in recorded history appearing three times the size of Venus, about 16 times brighter than Venus and considered about 7200 light years from the Earth. The site of a giant pole that stood at Mound 72 aligns with the coordinates of where the supernova shined in both the night and day sky for three years.

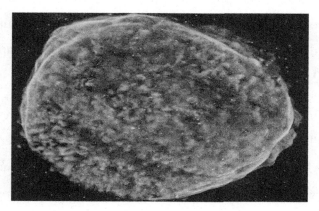

SN 1006   -7.5 visual magnitude

The Cahokia culture was known as Mound Builders who constructed earthen mounds utilized for ceremonial and burial purposes. They built 190 mounds in platform, ridge-top, and circular shapes aligned to a planned city grid which was orientated five degrees east of the north. The alignment focuses on the summer solstice sunrise and the southern maximum moonrise, orientating Cahokia to the movement of both the sun and the moon. Today eighty mounds still remain because of the technique used in finishing them with hard black clay which protected them from erosion.

The layout and structures of Cahokia are almost identical to some Mayan cities. Archeologists uncovered tools, elaborate ceramics, finely sculptured stoneware, carefully embossed engraved copper and mica sheets and tri-notched projectile points strikingly similar to that culture indicating that there was a strong Mayan influence. It is thought that perhaps there was a trade route to Mexico City with the Mississippi River providing a direct waterway.

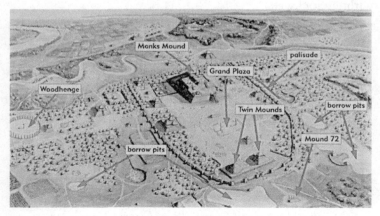

Present day layout of Cahokia

Monks Mound – Mound 38

Monks Mound, Mound 38, named after French Trappist Monks who once settled nearby, is the center of the site and is the largest Pre-Columbian structure north of the Valley of Mexico. It is a four-terraced platform mound that is 100 feet high, 951 feet long, 836 feet wide, covering 13.8 acres, and contains about 814,000 cubic yards of earth. It was topped by a structure thought to have measured 105 feet in length, and 48 feet in width, and been as much as 50 feet high, making its peak 150 feet about the level of the plaza that was constructed entirely of basket-transported soil and clay. It is roughly the same size as the Great Pyramid of Giza and thought to have been a ritual space. Upon reaching the top, there is a vibration or "vortex" emanating from the middle of the mound. A vortex is a small area of energy swirling clockwise.

Monks Mound – Mound 38 © Cheryl Lynn Carter

Woodhenge – Mound 72

Approximately 2,790 feet south of Monks Mound is Mound 72. The area of 412 feet appears to have begun as a circle of forty-eight large upright wooden posts resembling Stonehenge which archeologists have named Woodhenge. It was discovered that four of the posts were at pivotal locations marking the north, south, east, and west. The East and west marked the equinox sunrise and sunsets. Four others were noted to mark the summer solstice sunrise and sunset and the winter solstice sunrise and sunset positions. Archeologists used Radiocarbon dating to place the construction date to the Lohmann Phase 1000-1050 A.D. Excavations indicate that it could have been a series of smaller mounds that were then reshaped and covered over to give the mound its final shape. Later, Woodhenge was removed and a series of mortuary houses, mass burials, and eventually the ridge top mound were erected in its place.

Woodhenge – Mound 72 © Cheryl Lynn Carter

Interesting heart-shape in the rings of the wood
© Cheryl Lynn Carter

The Birdman

One of the posts that marked the summer solstice sunrise was nearest to the burial of what is known as "the Birdman." Four male skeletons surrounded the center burial; one merely bones, two others lay flat, and the fourth face down with one of its legs up to its chest. They were buried with ceramics, gaming stones, copper covered shafts, jewelry, and artifacts that have been traced as far away as Oklahoma.

In the center were the remains of a male and female. The man, thought to be someone of high ranking such as a chief, laid on an elevated platform, was tall and in his forties with his feet pointing toward the northwest. He rested upon a bed of 20,000 marine shell disc beads that formed the shape of a falcon. The bird's head was beneath his and its wings and tail beneath his arms and legs. Buried beneath the man was a woman who was face down. It is believed that the four men were "retainers" who were a human sacrifice for nobility in order to continue to serve him in the afterlife. The woman was most likely the man's wife who chose to sacrifice herself for her dead husband.

Mound 72 - Bird Man Grave
© Cahokia Mounds Historic Site

Archeologists theorize that the Beaded Burial was homage to the mystical Birdman, a legendary falcon warrior hero whose beaked face has appeared on many artifacts from Cahokia. The Birdman is a heroic figure whose twin sons fought off a race of Giants.

The Birdman Tablet made of sandstone measures four inches by two. It is believed to represent the Sky World, Human World, and the Underworld. The Cahokia people were thought to have communicated with the "gods" who descended from the Sky World.

Birdman Tablet Front   Reverse© Cheryl Lynn Carter

The Birdman Tablet actually represents a sky map from the year 500 A.D. The Astronomer Surveyor is at mid heaven. His right eye is at Ursa Minor, the North Pole Star, and his heart is in Cahokia at the Ursa Major position. His earring repesents Woodhenge at the celestial meridian.

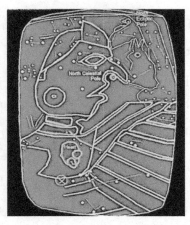

Birdman Tablet – Sky Map

All together archeologists found 270 people interred in the mound. It was discovered that 62% of them were sacrificial victims based on signs of ritual execution and method of burial. Four young males were missing their hands and skulls. There was a mass grave of more than fifty young women around age twenty-one and another mass grave containing forty men who appear to have been violently killed with some perhaps burned alive. From the vertical position of some of the fingers which appear to have been digging in the sand, it is apparent that not all the victims were dead when they were interred.

Mound 96

Mound 96 is a small mound just north east of Mound 72 approximately forty-nine feet wide at its base with a projecting ramp on its eastern side giving it a t-shape. It was built around the location of the winter sunset pole of the Woodhenge and orientated along the north-south and east-west alignment common at Cahokia with the ramp facing the winter solstice pole. It is believed to be the location of a charnel or mortuary house. This is a term given to an area surrounded by wood, stone, or earthwork barrier in which the dead bodies are placed for excarnation and to await a secondary or collective burial. Excarnation is an archeology term also known as defleshing which is the practice of removing the flesh and organs of the dead before burial leaving only the bones.

Mound 96 © Cheryl Lynn Carter

The Rattlesnake Causeway

An ancient road, which Archeologists are calling the Rattlesnake Causeway, is an elevated embankment about 26 feet wide and reaches from Cahokia's Grand Plaza south through the center of the city where it dead ends in the middle of a burial mound known as Rattlesnake Mound. The mound is about five feet long, two hundred feet wide, and thirty feet in height. It is thought that the roadway is both a literal and symbolic center of the city as it is aligned five degrees east of north forming a central axis around which the city is built. Research has discovered that Cahokia's buildings align with a celestial event known as the Lunar Standstill when the moon rises at the southern most point in the sky. The event occurs once every 18.6 years, and as seen from the Grand Plaza, it is visible over the bluffs of Rattlesnake Mound where the causeway ends. The mound contains 140 interments and is halfway down the road from Mound 72. Archeologists suggest that it served as sort of a conduit between the realms of the living and the dead.

For unknown reasons, the Cahokia culture appeared to have collapsed between 1400-1500 A.D. Archeologists speculated that the people may have depleted the area of resources such as over farming, cutting down all the trees, over hunting, or over fishing. There is also evidence that suggests the area was severely flooded twice once between 1100-1260 and again between 1340-1460. Another time there was a catastrophic drought. Perhaps a combination of these factors led them to abandon Cahokia.

The Illinois Confederation migrated to southern Illinois around 1500 A.D. They spoke an Algonquian language of Miami-Illini and had most likely migrated from eastern areas where the Algonquian language tribes emerged along the Atlantic Coast and waterways. The name Illinois derives its name from the Illiniwek Confederation of tribes that included Cahokia, Kaskaskia, Michigamea, Moingwena, Peoria, and Tamaroa from the word "illiniwek" meaning "he speaks in an ordinary way." Structures built by them included stone forts or "pounds."

Giant City Stone Fort

One such site is the Giant City Stone Fort which is now located within the Giant City State Park in Makanda, Illinois. The fort dates back to the late Woodland period of 600-900 A.D. It is one of ten such sites known in southern Illinois that were constructed on hilltops or bluffs. Giant City sits atop a sloped eighty foot sandstone cliff made of Pennsylvanian-aged Makanda Sandstone. This sandstone was carved 20,000 years ago by the melting waters of a Pleistocene glacier that stopped a mere 1.5 miles from the park. The ruins consist of a series of broken stone sections that extend from east to west through the Freeman Run Valley. The original stone wall was at one time 285 feet long, 6 feet high, and 9 feet thick. It is thought to have been a gathering place perhaps for trading or ceremony. In 1987, it was placed on the National Registry of Historic Places.

Giant City Stone Fort

New Madrid Fault

Amidst all the beauty of the Earth, there are times when she can be an unforgiving. One such occasion was on December 16, 1811, at 2:15 a.m. when a great earthquake estimated to have been 8.0 on the Richter Scale, was reported along the New Madrid Fault. It was so violent that it caused the Mississippi River to flow backward momentarily and change its course in several spots. At 12:00 a.m. the following day, a 7.4 aftershock followed. These events remain the most powerful earthquakes to hit the contiguous United States east of the Rocky Mountains in recorded history.

It is estimated that these earthquakes were felt over roughly one million square miles. The 1906 San Francisco earthquake by comparison was felt 6,200 square miles. Then on January 23, 1812, another 7.6 earthquake hit at 9:00 a.m. A week later on February 7, 1812, at 3:45 a.m. there was an 8.0 earthquake that created waterfalls on the Mississippi River followed by a 7.5 aftershock at 10:40 p.m.

The New Madrid Fault extends through five states, stretches southward from Cairo, Illinois, through Hayli, Caruthersville and New Madrid in Missouri, through Blytheville and into Marked Tree, Arkansas. The fault is a 150 mile long seismic zone that is still a threat to the region today.

213

The underlying cause appears to be related to an ancient geological feature buried under the Mississippi River alluvial plain known as the Reelfoot Rift. The New Madrid Seismic Zone is made up of reactivated faults that formed when what is now North America began to split apart during the breakup of the supercontinent Rodenia in the Neoproterozic Era about 750 million years ago. Faults were created along the rift rocks and igneous rocks formed from magna that was being pushed towards the surface.

Murphysboro Mud Monster "Big Muddy"

For approximately fourteen days in the summer of 1973, a huge, hairy, albino creature terrorized the small town of Murphysboro. It became known as the Murphysboro Mud Monster or Big Muddy.

On June 25, 1973, around midnight a young couple was parked near the Muddy River for a romantic evening. Randy Needham and Judy Johnson had selected the secluded location just near the woods to carry on their relationship as her father had strictly forbidden them to see each other. They had been listening to the radio and talking when they heard a horrific shriek almost like that of an eagle. Needham turned down the radio and they listened. A few seconds later they heard another shriek. When he turned on his headlights, they saw a huge, foul smelling creature emerge from the woods and heading toward them. They quickly drove away, neither of them speaking about what had just happened, and then stopped in town.

Both of them agreed that they should make a report with the police even though Johnson knew this would mean her father finding about their secret romance. They gave a detailed account describing the creature that looked like an over-sized gorilla, about eight feet tall with matted, mud streaked fur. It appeared to have been walking on two legs. The police immediately dispatched two officers to investigate the sighting.

Officers Meryl Lindsay and Jimmy Nash searched the area with flashlights and spotted tracks in the mud that were approximately 3-4 inches deep, 10-12 inches long, and 3 inches wide. While they continued their search, the heard a strange scream come from the woods. Whatever had made the sound had to be no more than 300 feet away from them. They went back to the station and returned with Officer Bob Scote to photograph the footprints. Upon discovering more footprints, they followed them tracing their path along the river. Suddenly 100 yards away, they heard the terrifying scream. They quickly abandoned their search, retreated to the car, watched, and waited. After awhile, they got back out and continued their pursuit for the remainder of the night attempting to track down a splashing sound they heard which sounded like something big running through the knee deep water. Unfortunately, they never located the mysterious creature.

At 10:30 p.m. on June 26, five year old Christian Barel was playing in his backyard which was relatively close to the Big Muddy River. Suddenly, he noticed a huge white shape emerging from behind the fence that separated his yard from the neighbor's. Startled, he dropped the mason jar that he was using to catch fireflies and ran inside. He began telling his father that there was a big white ghost in the backyard. At first his father was skeptical until he talked with the neighbors on the other side of the fence.

Ten minutes later, Randy and Cheryl Creath were sitting on their back porch when they heard something rustling in the bushes about fifteen feet away from them. Ray turned on the porch light to get a better look, but saw nothing. Thinking it was kids, they started out to find them. They hadn't gone far when they came face to face with a huge creature. They described it as being 7 feet tall, ape-like, about

350 pounds, long white fur like a sheep dog that was matted, and glowing red eyes.

Ten days later on July 4, a traveling carnival had stopped and set up camp in Riverside Park a place near the river just below Ray's house. They had been unaware of whatever had been lurking around. At 2:00 a.m. on July 7 after the carnival had closed down, three carnies Otis Norvis, Wesley Lavender, and Ray Adkerson were sitting behind one of the trucks. Suddenly, they heard the Shetland ponies begin to whine. They appeared very upset, almost terrorized, tugging at their ropes desperately trying to get away; away from the 8 foot, 400 pound creature covered with fur calming watching the ponies with his head cocked to the side in an almost curious pose. The men chased it away and it ran toward the woods.

Big Muddy

The Enfield Horror

The Enfield Horror of Enfield, Illinois, is probably one of the strangest cryptid encounters ever recorded. On April 25, 1973, a ten year old boy named Greg Garrett claimed to have been attacked by a mysterious creature as he was playing in his backyard. It was four feet tall, had three legs, grayish slimy skin, short claws, and huge red eyes. The creature approached him and stomped on his feet tearing his tennis shoes to shreds.

A half hour later, neighbors Henry Mc Daniel and his wife had returned home only to find their two children Henry Jr. and Lil very frightened. They said they heard scratching sounds as if some huge animal was trying to break into the house. Henry naturally assumed it was probably a dog so he went outside to take a look around. When he opened the door, he saw the same creature sitting on the stoop. He quickly shut the door and ran for his .22 pistol. He went back out and shot at it, but the creature only hissed. Then it ran off covering an area about fifty feet in a series of only three leaps before disappearing into the brush near the L & N Railroad embankment.

Henry notified the police and they came to the house a few minutes later. He described to them a creature standing four feet tall, with three legs, grayish slimy skin, claws and red eyes the size of flashlights. When they inspected the property, they found dog-like prints in the yard. However, there were six toe pads by what appeared to be a three footed animal with two measuring four inches and the third slightly smaller.

Henry McDaniel Home

On May 6, Henry was awakened by the howls of the neighborhood dogs. As he opened the front door to see what the commotion was all about, he again saw the same creature moving along the railroad tracks.

The last witness of the Enfield Horror was Rich Rainbow the news director of radio station WWKI. He and three others claimed to see the strange creature in the same area. They didn't get a chance to photograph it, but they did manage to tape record the monster's disturbing scream.

Noted cryptozoologist Loren Coleman also went to investigate the area. He too heard the haunting cries describing them as banshee-like sounds. In July 1974, Fate Magazine featured a story by him and Jerome Clark entitled "Swamp Slobs Invade Illinois."

The Enfield Horror ended as abruptly as it began. Some Ufologists speculate it was related to extraterrestrial activity that was reported in the area at the same time. So was it alien, interdimensional, or a genetic mutation?

Enfield Horror

St. Clair Triangle

Within the Little Egypt Triangle, is another mysterious area known as the St. Clair Triangle where one day several eye witnesses reported seeing a massive triangular craft in the early morning sky. This was observed in Lebanon, Highland, Dupo, Shiloh, Summerfield, Millstadt, and O'Fallon. Among them were some very credible witnesses, a business owner and four police officers. The incident soon caught the attention of the media and several news stories covered the event including "UFOs Over Illinois" on the Discovery Channel and an independent documentary titled "The Edge of Reality: Illinois UFO January 5, 2000."

It was a cold morning on January 5, 2000, when at 4:00 a.m. Melvern Noll went to inspect his miniature golf course to determine if there was any damage to his heating system. Satisfied that all was well, he got back into his truck and was about to drive away when he noticed a bright light shining down towards the ground. As he watched, it came closer to him and then he saw red lights shining down on the ground. He looked up into the sky to see what looked like a bright star. As it came closer, about 800-1000 feet above him, he saw it was some sort of craft as large as a football field, that appeared to have two floors with windows that were brightly lit inside. It was moving slowly about 50 mph in a northeast direction and not making any sound. He was fearful that nobody would believe his story, but reported it to the police. Dispatch immediately sent out an officer to investigate.

At 4:12 a.m. as Officer Ed Barton approached the area, he saw a massive, elongated, triangle shaped craft in the sky. It was about 75 feet in length and 40 feet wide. At each corner, was a massive bright white light and a smaller flashing red light was on the bottom. The rear of the craft had an array of white lights across the side and a thin strip of multicolored lights that ran horizontally. It was approximately 1000 feet above the ground and not making a sound. As he watched it, it began rotating in the sky as if to turn. However, it did not bank like any regular aircraft. Instead, it pivoted in mid air without ever tilting to one side or the other and remained completely level.

At 4:23 a.m. Officer Dave Martin observed an object hovering at an altitude of about 1000 feet above the ground. It did not make any sound and resembled the shape of a very large triangle about 75-100 yards wide. Three brilliant lights were being projected downward from the craft and small red and green lights were on the back end. The bottom did not appear to be a flat surface; one section was lower than another section. He recalled there being some detail on the bottom of the craft similar to building blocks.

At 4:28 a.m. Officer Craig Stevens spotted an object in the sky at an altitude of about 500-1000 feet. It was silent and was V-shaped with a concave rear with s horizontally moving strobing white light. The entire rear surface consisted of a bank of white lights similar to the description of the others and the texture of the craft was compared to the three dimensional blockiness of a naval battleship.

Then at 5:03 a.m. Officer Matt Jany observed a craft hovering approximately 1000 feet above the ground. It was triangular shaped with lights that were brighter than a typical aircraft. It was silent with large red glowing lights on the underside accompanied by white lights which were flashing around the crafts perimeter.

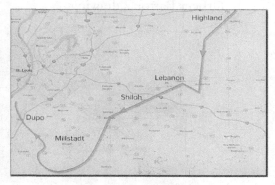

Flight Pattern of the UFO

Officer Craig Stevens   Officer Ed Barton
Riverfront Times, St. Louis

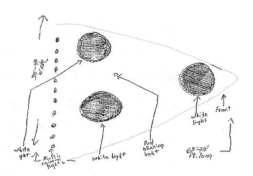

Officer Barton's drawing

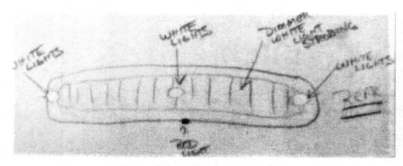

Officer Steven's drawing of the rear

St. Clair County
Emergency Services *and* **Disaster Agency**

Central Communications (CENCOM), Public Safety Answering Point

Coordinator · Belleville, IL 62220-1193 · (618
FAX#

PSAP Manager

To: Darryl Barker

From:

Date: January 5, 2000

Radio transmission's between CENCOM, Lebanon PD, Shiloh, PD, Millstadt PD, and Dupo PD.

4:11:58	CENCOM advises Lebanon PD that Highland PD has identified a UFO heading toward Lebanon
4:13:40	Lebanon officer acknowledges CENCOM
4:16:00	Traffic between CENCOM and Lebanon PD
4:18:31	Lebanon officer advises CENCOM he has identified a UFO
4:21:00	Lebanon officer asks CENCOM to contact Scott Air Force Base if they have any planes in the area.
4:23:06	Lebanon officer advises CENCOM UFO is west bound close to Scott Air Force Base
4:23:57	Shiloh Officer possibly identifies the UFO
4:24:44	Lebanon officer goes back in service
4:29:50	Transmission between Lebanon Officer and Shiloh Officer
4:39:27	Millstadt officer notifies CENCOM he has sighted the UFO
4:40:43	Millstadt Officer describes UFO
5:03:32	Millstadt Officer asks Dupo Officer if he has a Polaroid camera
5:03:36	Dupo Officer advises Millstadt officer he has sighted the UFO
5:42:10	CENCOM requests Millstadt Officer to contact Shiloh officer

Report between CENCOM
Central Communications and Police

Millstadt Enterprise Journal – January 19, 2000

NIDS Ongoing Investigation Into Major Illinois Police UFO Sighting

From Colm Kelleher <nids@anv.net>
Complete Ongoing NIDS Investigation At:
http://www.accessnv.com/nids
1-18-2000

The National Institute for Discovery Science (NIDS) 24-hour hot line (702-798-1700) received a report at 3:46 am Pacific time on 1/5/2000 from a police officer at Milstadt, Illinois. The officer reported an unidentified flying object seen by a business owner and several police officers at Lebanon, Millstadt, Shiloh and Dupo, Illinois. The report to NIDS came approximately two hours after the sighting.

After multiple telephone calls to the locale, NIDS dispatched two investigators to the location to conduct face-to-face interviews with eyewitnesses. The following can be summarized from the interview transcripts:

The civilian, who had driven to his miniature golf course in Highland at 4:01 AM, reported an object like "a floating house with very bright internal lights flying at a low altitude from northeast and moving southwest. The object was two to three stories high and was the length of a football field. The eyewitness immediately drove to the Highland PD and reported the sighting. The police dispatcher from Highland contacted The Central Communications dispatcher from St. Clair County, who in turn requested the Lebanon Police Department to look out for the object.

NIDS National Institute For Discovery Science Report

Other Sightings

Earlier in March 1967, Leona Boeving and her daughter watched from their window and observed a strange craft that had landed in a field near her farm in New Baden. She described it as looking like the full moon was cut in half standing on the ground. It had a bright white light on the top and an entire row of small red lights at the bottom. There were metallic stripes of silver around it. Afterward when they explored the field, the heat from the craft had left burn marks on the ground. Nothing was able to grow there for awhile.

On July 4, 1997, there was a mass sighting of a bright blue light the size of a basketball sailing from east to west across the sky between 9:30-10:00 p.m. It was seen in Bellville, Fairview Heights, Mascoutah, Trenton, Troy, Hamel, Praroe Du Rocher, and Greenville. Then again on July 8, 1997, reporter Brian Brueggemann watched as a group of blue lights hovered low in a field.

The Alton Piasa

In 1673, Jesuit missionary Jacques Marquette and Louis Joliet were exploring the Mississippi valley region in a canoe outside of what is now Alton, when they came upon a huge drawing one hundred feet above on the limestone cliffs. What they saw cut a half inch into the rock and painted red, black, and blue was some sort of creature. It had the head of a bear, face somewhat like a man, horns of an elk, scaly body of a fish, legs like a bear, eagle claws, and a fifty foot long tail that wound three times around the body. But who was responsible for this drawing on a cliff so high that it would be almost impossible for a man to climb?

Along the Mississippi valley where its banks form the boundary between Illinois and Missouri, there can be found thousands of ancient carvings and pictographs beneath overhanging cliffs and on the walls of caves. It was here that the Cahokia people painted numerous serpents, dragons, and monstrous birds on the limestone. The most famous of the cliff drawings is what is known as the Piasa. Measuring an astounding thirty feet wide and twelve feet high, this is the largest pictograph ever recorded in aboriginal America. The word Piasa comes from the Illini meaning "one that devours men." Was the Piasa a mystical creature that the Cahokia revered, was it a prehistoric bird, or does it still actually exist?

Piasa on the cliff

In the 1940's, many sightings of huge birds were reported in and around Alton not far from the Piasa image. On April, 4, 1948, Army Colonel Walter F. Siegmund observed a massive bird flying northeast that at first he thought might have been a glider. Additional mass sightings of huge birds were reported on April 10 and 24. Flight instructors at a local airport observed a large bird that had cast a shadow as big as a Piper Club aircraft from 500 feet up. Then as quick as they had appeared, the huge birds were gone never to be seen again.

Murders in Little Egypt

Dr. John Dale Cavaness was a small town family physician and chief surgeon at Pearce Hospital. He was known for the professional manner in which he cared for his patients, sometimes making house calls, and often waiving his fees for anyone who was unable to pay for his services. He was also known for the "Murders in Little Egypt."

In 1951, Dale met a nurse named Marian Newberry and they married the following year. Together they had three sons Mark, Sean, and Kevin. They had a beautiful home and livestock farm in Eldorado. Everything about their life resembled a Norman Rockwell painting, but behind closed doors it was something entirely different. Dale was a womanizer and a drinker; a very angry drinker. He would verbally abuse and beat his wife and children.

In 1972, his drinking caused an automobile accident that claimed the lives of a father and his baby. His cold comment to the police was, "Everybody's gotta die sometime." Somehow, his only punishment was two years probation and a $1000 fine. Fearing for her life and that of the boys, Marian finally found the courage to leave him taking the boys to St. Louis, Missouri.

Mark didn't take the divorce very well. He began hanging out with the wrong crowd, drinking, smoking pot, and eventually dropping out of school. By the time he was 22, he was struggling with life's challenges so he moved back with his father and worked on the farm.

On Easter Sunday in 1977, he agreed to meet with his mother and younger brothers and return to St. Louis. When they arrived at the farm, there was no answer when they knocked on the door of his trailer. Sean walked over by his Jeep and discovered his brother's body in the tall grass. Even though the coroner determined the time of death to be around twelve hours ago, there wasn't much flesh remaining as animals had scavenged his body. It was uncertain how the cause of death was determined to be suicide. Nonetheless, Dale collected $40,000 in life insurance on his son.

Although Dr. Cavaness was said to be a millionaire, he rarely had enough money. Instead, he devised a plan to live off insurance policies. It began in 1971, when he received a $100,000 payment for the loss of his home in a fire. In 1973, he was awarded $86,000 when another one of his properties caught fire. Then in 1980 desperate for money again, he convinced Sean and Kevin to participate in an insurance scheme. He explained to them how easily they could borrow against the policy if they wanted. He paid the monthly premiums and claimed them as tax deductions, but that was not enough.

On December 14, 1980, Sean's body was discovered in a remote area of St. Louis by a farmer. He had been shot in the head twice with a .357 Magnum. When questioned, Dale told the police he hadn't seen Sean for a long time. But when witnesses said they saw the two of them together that night, he changed his story. He said they had been out drinking that night when Sean asked to see his pistol. Thinking nothing about it, he handed it to him. Sean pointed the gun to the back of his head and pulled the trigger. Again, Dr. Cavaness collected $148, 000 insurance on another son.

However, this time the police conducted a more thorough investigation and arrested him for murder. And yet still popular with businessmen and his patients, his supporters set up a defense fund for his trial. However, no amount of money could dispute the evidence and on January 6, 1981, he was at last convicted of murder.

Dr. John Dale Cavaness

Southern Illinoisan – December 20, 1984

Chapter 8
Nevada Triangle

Nevada derives its name from the Spanish word "nevada" meaning "snow-clad" in reference to the high snow covered mountains of it's mostly desert terrain. The Paleo people or "ancient ones" first inhabited this area in about 3000 B.C where they hunted the Great Mammoth. In the following years, the Washoe or "people from here" occupied the Sierra Nevada Mountain Range, the Paiute or "water" resided in northern and southern Nevada, and the Shoshone or "the people" lived in the west.

As Spanish settlers journeyed west, they claimed the land now known as Nevada, to be part of the Viceroyalty of New Spain. Upon gaining its independence in 1821, it became part of Mexico until in 1848, after the victory in the Mexican-American War, where as the United States laid claim to the land making it part of the Utah Territory.

Latter-Day Saints

Joseph Smith was the Prophet and founder of the Church of Jesus Christ Latter-Day Saints. In 1839, he brought his followers to a small town called Commerce, Illinois and renamed it Nauvoo, a Hebrew word meaning "beautiful place." Although Nauvoo was an ideal place, he had a dream of something better, a location they might self-govern being free from the restrictions of the United States government. During meetings of the Council of 50, the basis for the government of the State of Deseret was formed. He chose the name "Deseret" from a passage in the Book of Mormon. "And they did also carry with them deseret." – Ether 2:3

Deseret was the honey bee in the language of the Jadeites who led the people after the Tower of Babble. He chose this name as a representation of industry and how he perceived this new state would become. He instilled in his followers how they should be as productive and self-reliant as the honey bee.

However, before he could fulfill his dream of this place, on June 27, 1844, a mob shot and killed him. So with a preponderance of reasons, Brigham Young, his successor, concluded Illinois was no longer a suitable place to live and

235

proposed they journey west to the Mexico Territory immediately.

In 1847, Brigham Young along with a group of scouts, and 145 church members proceeded to make a westward exodus in hopes of locating a remote area where the church might seek refuge from the United States government. The arduous journey of 1,300 miles took 111 days before they reached they finally reached the valley of the Great Salt Lake on July, 24, 1947. Just four days after arriving, he selected the future location of the Salt Lake Temple.

Joseph Smith   Brigham Young

William Hamblin, was called upon to serve a mission to the Southern Paiute. He was shown a location where an abundance of a shiny element that the people called panacker was present. "Pan-nuc-ker" means "metal, wealth." He recognized it as silver and in 1864 he established the Panacker Ledge claim. It was the first mine in Nevada.

Panacker Ledge Claim

Nevada is officially known as the Silver State because of the significance that silver had to its history. A lode of ore was discovered under the east slope of Mount Davidson, a peak in the Virginia Range. In 1859, the Comstock Lode, deep under Virginia City, was the first major discovery of silver ore in the United States and was named after Henry Comstock.

237

Henry Comstock

Henry, born in Ontario, came west seeking a job as a sheep herder. He was often described as self-righteous, over-bearing and quite lazy. Those who knew him best called him "Pancake" because he was too lazy and impatient to bake bread preferring the quick and easy flapjack. One day, he traded in an old blind horse and a bottle of whiskey for a share in the claim at Gold Hill, a mine near a Cornish town.

In 1859 after the discovery of ore, true to his nature, he insisted that his partners name the mine after him. Unfortunately, neither he nor his partners had the money or expertise to properly work the mine so they all eventually sold their part of the claim. He sold his interest early for $11,000 which was a remarkable sum at the time and never did profit from it. The mine later produced over $10 million in profits. Penniless in 1870, he committed suicide by his own pistol.

Nevada is also known for the advancement in mining technology that it spurred; square set timbering and the Washoe process for extracting silver from ore. In 1852 at age nineteen, Philip Deidesheimer from Darmstadt, Hesse, Germany emigrated to California. He attended the prestigious Freeberg University of Mining where he became a mining engineer. In 1860, he was hired by W.F. Babcock a trustee of the Ophir Mine which was a part of the Comstock Lode. It was here that he solved one of the mine's most crucial engineering needs.

Inside the Comstock mines, the rock was soft and easily collapsed into the working cavities where the ore was being extracted. In addition, the presence of clay would swell greatly upon being exposed to the air causing great pressure that the mine timbering of that time could not support. Inspired by the structure of honeycombs, he designed square timbering. This was a system using heavy timber cubes as supports for underground mining tunnels and shafts that enabled the miners to open three dimensional cavities of any size. In large openings, the cubes were filled with the waste rock creating a solid pillar of wood and rock from floor to roof. The square set timbering system slowed the swelling action just long enough for the ore extraction.

In 1849 Almarin B. Paul hearing about the discovery of gold in California, left his home in New Jersey and headed west. There he opened a mercantile store and operated it until 1850 when he turned his interest to mining. He later moved to Nevada City where he built one of the first mills in Nevada County. It was here that he noticed the processing method was not economical and became strongly impressed with the necessity of improving the process. The Freiberg Process or pan amalgamation process was devised in 1609 in Germany. It is a method of extracting silver from ore using salt (sodium sulfate), bluestone (copper sulfate) and mercury and heating it in shallow copper vessels.

In 1868, he secured patents and devised the Washoe Process naming it after the area once inhabited by the Washoe tribe. Instead of using shallow pans, iron tanks with mechanical agitators held 1,200 to 1,500 pounds of ore that had been crushed to sand size. Water was added to make a pulp along with sixty to seventy pounds of mercury, three pounds of sodium sulfate and three pounds of copper sulfate. A circular iron plate called a muller was mounted on a vertical shaft and lowered into the tank and was rotated to provide both agitation and additional grinding. Heat was delivered to the tanks by steam pipes. This new process reduced the working time from thirty days to four hours.

Samuel Clemens

In the summer of 1861, twenty-five year old Samuel Clemens decided to move west in order to work with his brother Orion who had just been appointed Secretary of the Nevada Territory. However, soon after arriving in Carson City, Nevada, he lost interest in working under his brother and shifted his focus to trying to strike it rich as a miner. Unfortunately, he soon realized that many others shared his dream and the work was hard with little reward. So once again he looked for another avenue of work and inquired about working as a newspaper reporter. Shortly afterward, he was offered an editor position at the Virginia City Daily Territorial Enterprise. Along with his regular reporting of the news he wrote humorous and satirical letters for the newspaper. It was in a letter published on February 3, 1863, where he first signed "Mark Twain" to his work and would continue to write under that pseudonym.

Samuel Clemens – Mark Twain

Before coming to Nevada, Samuel was a licensed steamboat pilot. One of the duties of the crewmen was to test the depth of the water assuring the boat would be able to navigate safely through. Depth was measured by means of a sounding line which was a length of thin rope with a plummet made of lead at its end. It was cast into the water and measurements were made. The crewman would shout out, "deep six" meaning six fathoms which is a maritime unit of depth equivalent to six feet or "by the mark of the twain," an old English word for two, meaning the mark on the line was two fathoms.

The Nevada Triangle

Sprawled out over a vast expanse of desolate landscape of desert and mountains is an area known as the Nevada Triangle. It spans from Las Vegas, Nevada in the Southeast to Fresno, California in the west, and to Reno, Nevada at the top. The Sierra Nevada stretches 400 miles from Nevada to California and lies directly within the mysterious triangle. Lake Tahoe was formed when the eruptions from the now extinct volcano Mount Pluto created a dam forming the largest alpine lake in North America. An alpine lake is considered a lake at a high altitude starting at 5,000 feet above sea level.

Nevada Triangle

The Nevada Triangle is also known as the Graveyard for Airplanes. The most famous place where planes have gone missing is the Bermuda Triangle. However, the total number of aircraft that have been reported missing in the Nevada Triangle have greatly outnumbered those that have been reported in the Bermuda Triangle where there have been thirty unsolved cases of aircraft disappearances since the late 1800's. That's a very small number compared to the 2000 vanished planes in the Nevada Triangle in just the last sixty years. Many of these planes were flown by experienced pilots.

One of the earliest reported incidents was in 1943 when a B-24E Liberator Bomber disappeared in the Sierra Nevada Mountains. The plane, part of the U.S. Army Air Corps 461st Bomb Group, 765th Bomb Squadron, took flight on December 5 and was piloted by 2nd Lieutenant Charles Willis Turvey and co-pilot 2nd Lieutenant Robert M. Hester. It also carried four other crew members including 2nd Lieutenant William Thomas Cronin serving as navigator; 2nd Lieutenant Ellis H. Fish, bombardier; Sergeant Robert Bursey, engineer; and Sergeant Howard A. Wandtke, radio operator. The flight was on a routine night training mission that began from Fresno, California, to Bakersfield, California, then to Tucson, Arizona, and back.

An extensive search mission began the following day when nine B-24 Bombers were sent out to locate the missing plane. However, instead of locating it, yet another bomber went missing. On the morning of December 6, 1943, Squadron Commander William Darden lifted off along with eight other B-24's. Captain Darden, his plane, and crew were not seen again until 1955 when Huntington Lake Reservoir was drained for repairs to the dam.

The investigation into the loss of the bomber stated that Captain Darden had experienced high wind turbulence and began to lose hydraulic pressure. When he saw what appeared to be a snow-covered clearing, he instructed his crew to bail out, but only two jumped. The investigation further stated that the pilot may have mistaken the frozen lake for a clearing, however, the two men who had parachuted from the plane and survived made statements that the lake was not frozen. When the plane was finally discovered, it was resting 190 feet below the water with its five crew members still at their stations.

Hawthorne Nevada Airlines Flight 708

Hawthorne Nevada Airlines Douglas DC-3, Flight 708, tail number N15570, nicknamed the Gambler's Special was a domestic non-scheduled passenger flight between Hawthorne, Nevada, and Holly-Wood Burbank, California.

On February 18, 1969, they departed at 3:50 a.m. PST with the flight crew of Captain Fred Hall, First Officer Raymond Hamer, and one flight attendant Patricia Nannes. At 4:06 a.m. the pilot contacted the Tonopah Flight Service Station asking for clearance from air traffic control in order to operate using visual flight rules instead of instrument flight rules because the skies were clear. That was the last transmission.

Tonopah tracked the plane flying a pattern over Owens Valley in Inyo County, California indicating the pilot must have chosen an alternate route in order to avoid the mountains surrounding Hawthorne. Sixteen minutes into their flight, the plane was declared missing along with the thirty-two passengers and three crew members.

Snow and dangerous mountainous terrain hampered the search efforts and during the search, an Air Force helicopter crashed. On August 8, 1969, the wreckage was finally discovered. The plane had hit a sheer cliff face on the east side of Mount Whitney at 11,770 feet. The cause of the crash was undetermined as there was no evidence of any mechanical or electrical malfunction.

Hawthorne Flight 708 – N15570

Crash Site

File No. 3-2594

NATIONAL TRANSPORTATION SAFETY BOARD
DEPARTMENT OF TRANSPORTATION
AIRCRAFT ACCIDENT REPORT

Adopted: February 5, 1970

MINERAL COUNTY AIRLINES,
d.b.a. HAWTHORNE NEVADA AIRLINES,
DC-3, N15570
NEAR LONE PINE, CALIFORNIA
FEBRUARY 18, 1969

SYNOPSIS

A Hawthorne-Nevada Airlines (HNVT), DC-3, N15570, operating as Flight 708, crashed approximately 11 nautical miles west of Lone Pine, California, about 0510 P.s.t., February 18, 1969. The 32 passengers and three crewmembers aboard the aircraft died in the accident, and the aircraft was destroyed.

The flight departed Hawthorne, Nevada, 0350 P.s.t., on February 18, 1969, on a VFR flight plan for Burbank and Long Beach, California. At 0406, Flight 708 contacted the Tonopah Flight Service Station on the Mina VOR frequency and activated a VFR flight plan which had previously been filed by telephone from Hawthorne, Nevada. No further contact was had with the flight. The aircraft was declared missing, and presumed down somewhere between Hawthorne, Nevada, and Burbank, California. Air and ground search operations were instituted, but due to heavy snows and inclement weather, the aircraft was not located. The crash site, approximately 11 nautical miles west of Lone Pine, California, was located August 8, 1969. The aircraft crashed on the east slope of Mount Whitney, at an elevation of approximately 11,770 feet. All persons on board the aircraft perished in the impact.

The Board determines that the probable cause of this accident was the deviation from the prescribed route of flight, as authorized in the company's FAA-approved operations specifications, resulting in the aircraft being operated under IFR weather conditions, in high mountainous terrain, in an area where there was a lack of radio navigation aids.

National Transportation Board
February 4, 1970 File No. 3-2594

Steve Fossett was a Chicago millionaire who was widely recognized for setting several aviation world records, as well as in 2002 being the first person to fly solo, non-stop, unrefueled around the world in a hot air balloon. At 8:45 a.m., on September 3, 2007, he took off from the Flying M Ranch owned by Barry Hilton which was about seventy miles from Reno. He was flying a single-engine Bellanca 8KCAB-180, a two-seat plane capable of aerobatic maneuvers, over Nevada's Great Basin Desert. He refrained from filling out a flight plan because he only intended to be gone about two hours.

When he failed to return, an extensive search was conducted. However, they found nothing and on September 15, 2008, he was declared dead. On September 29, a hiker discovered his identification card and pilot certificate in the Sierra Nevada Mountains in California near Minaret Summit. A few days later his plane was discovered approximately sixty-five miles from where he took off. Two bones recovered from the crash site were confirmed by DNA tests to be his.

Steve Fossett

Steve Fossett's plane

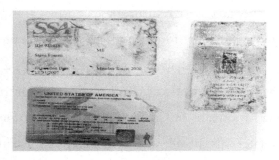

Soaring Society of America membership card,
Federal Aviation Administration card,
and Pilot's license Department of Aviation

So what could be the cause for all these disappearances? One theory relates to the somewhat unforgiving Sierra Nevada itself. The Sierra Nevada is a very remote area extending over 25,000 miles that consists of mountains and wilderness. There are some exceptionally high mountain peaks such as Mount Whitney with the highest point in the contiguous United States at 14,505 feet. Some believe that there is a natural phenomenon known as a "mountain wave" that may be causing all the planes to crash. This phenomenon is an airflow that is caused by unpredictable winds and downdrafts. When a downdraft occurs, it may cause a sudden and severe jolt followed by a lull and then more jolts which can come from all directions. Winds can sometimes rush down at four hundred feet per minute or more in the Sierra Nevadas and then bounce back up even faster. Another possible theory is that a plane might get too close to a certain government restricted area and mysteriously get shot down.

Groom Valley

Located within the Groom Valley of the Tonopah Basin is a salt flat. Its elevation is 4,409 feet, and it measures 3.7 miles from north to south and 3 miles from east to west, with a diameter of 11.3 miles. It is what remains of Lake Lahontan that was formed during the last glacial period about 12,700 years ago. The lake, once one of the largest in North America, had a surface of 8,500 square miles and a depth of 900 feet making it the size of Lake Erie. However, extreme climate changes about 9000 years ago caused the surface elevation to drop and the lake broke up into several small lakes. As in this case, the water in the desert heated and evaporated into vapor faster than it could be replenished by rain. The salt left behind formed a solid layer called a salt flat.

The discovery of silver ore in the Comstock Lode led prospectors to explore a remote area in Lincoln County, Nevada. In 1872, Jonas Brown Osborne and his partners secured a homestead of 400 acres and filed a claim to operate a mine, which they named Conception Mines, up on a mountainside overlooking this desolate dry lake bed. In 1876, the name was changed to Groom Nevada Lead Mines Company when additional financing was acquired from an English company called the Groom Lead Mines Limited.

Groom Nevada Lead Mine

Owner Name and Address			
Dan Sheahan	**International Mining Corporation**	**Sheahan Family**	**Vincent D. Miller Incorporated**
Nevada		Type Owner	Washington
Type Owner	Type Operator		Type Owner

Commodities

Additional textual information about a site or mine.

Commodity	Type	Importance
Lead	Metallic	Primary
Silver	Metallic	Primary
Copper	Metallic	Secondary
Gold	Metallic	Secondary
Zinc	Metallic	Secondary
Barium-Barite	Non-Metallic	Tertiary

Lincoln, Nevada
Current State

Continent	Country	State	County
North America	The United States	Nevada	Lincoln

Notes

NEAR SOUTH END OF GROOM RANGE. ON US AIR FORCE GUNNERY RANGE NOW. ON US AIR FORCE GUNNERY RANGE NOW. INFO FROM LAND ST. 1981.

Meridian / Township / Range Description

Meridian	Township	Section	Aliquot
Mount Diablo Meridian	T.7S R.35E	Sec. 11	
Mount Diablo Meridian	T.7S R.35E	Sec. 14	
Mount Diablo Meridian	T.7S R.35E	Sec. 3	

Groom Mine Deed – Patent 1661

In 1937, the mine was purchased by Patrick Sheahan and his brother who successfully worked the mine discovering lead, silver, copper, zinc, and gold. Then one day in 1941, the government sent surveyors to the region to search for a place in which they could test aerial gunnery and other weaponry. Dan and Horace Sheahan having realized they were not prepared to survive the very extreme elements and terrain invited the men to stay with them. Dan put them up in the bunkhouse, they ate with his family, and he even helped them survey the land.

But Dan soon discovered as the saying goes that "no good deed goes unpunished." Little did they know that on the salt flat just below them, the Nevada Test and Training Range would be testing the atomic bomb. The blast of the bombs blew out their windows and radioactive fallout caused some family members as well as horses to die.

In 1950, the roads leading to the mine were closed due to the secret military activities. This prompted Lincoln County and the family to build an alternate road from the east hoping this would avoid any further complications. However, soon after that the mill used to process ore mysteriously blew up.

In 1984, the government seized all the remaining land around the mine. Then they placed a security shack on Sheahan Blvd, the road the family had built for access to their property. This now required them to go through checkpoints and at times they even found themselves held at gunpoint as they tried to get to the mine.

The government's conundrum was how to handle this privately owned property that was situated dead center within a vast expanse of three million acres of government land. In 2014, the United States Department of Defense offered to purchase the property for 1.5 million dollars. When the family turned down the offer, in August 2015, it was raised to 5.2 million. But the Sheahan's stood steadfast contending that the property and future mineral discoveries were worth much more.

When negotiations had come to a standstill, on September 16, 2015, United States District Judge Miranda Du signed an order granting possession of the Groom Mine property to the United States government. The property was condemned under Eminent Domain citing the seizure of the property was in the best interest of top secret military operations. Although the Project Influence Rule applies where as the U.S. Constitution requires the government to pay just compensation, there has yet to be a fair settlement for the Sheahan family.

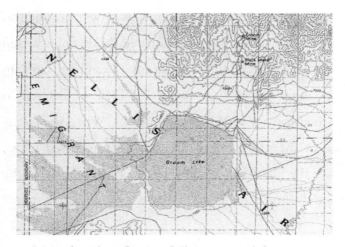

Map showing Groom Mine upper right corner
in reference to Nellis Air Base 37.3462°N 115.7692°W

Martha and Dan Sheahan
© Courtesy of the Sheanhan Family

Groom Mine @ Courtesy of the Sheahan Family

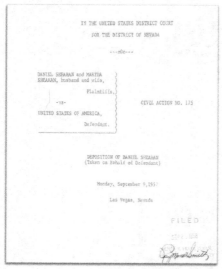

Deposition of Daniel Sheahan
September 9, 1957

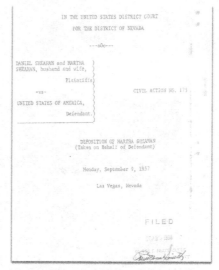

Deposition of Martha Sheahan
September 9, 1957

Area 51

Adjacent to Groom Lake is a sixty square mile area known by the ICAO Code of KXTA or Homey Airport, 37°14'0N 115°48'30W. At least that is what the government would like us to think. In a classified document during the Vietnam War, coincidentally it was referred to by another name "Area 51."

Area 51, a remote detachment of Edwards Air Force Base was established in 1955 by the Central Intelligence Agency to develop and test covert military aerospace technologies. Some of these projects resulted in the creation of the Lockheed F-117 Nighthawk, Archangel-12, and SR-71 Blackbird stealth planes. The F-117 Nighthawk was the first stealth aircraft designed to deflect radar detection. The AC-12 traveled at speeds of over 2000 mph and could traverse the continental United States in seventy minutes. The SR-71 was capable of flying at speeds over Mach 3.2 or 2,193.167 mph. and reaching a height of 85,000 feet.

Rectangular in shape, the restricted air space measures twenty-three by twenty-five miles. The area shares a border with the Yucca Flat and the Nevada Test Site, the location of nuclear tests conducted by the United States Department of Energy. Conspiracy Theorists claim that Area

51 is where the storage, examination, and reverse engineering of crashed alien spacecraft from Roswell took place.

On June 14, 1947, in Corona, about seventy-five miles north of Roswell, New Mexico, William Ware "Mac" Brazel the foreman of the J.B. Foster ranch and Timothy the son of his neighbor Floyd Proctor were out on horseback checking on his sheep after a bad thunder storm. It was here that they discovered a large amount of strange debris scattered around an area about 200 yards. He also noticed a shallow trench several hundred feet long that had been gorged into the ground. He wasn't sure what to think, but his main focus at the present was the sheep.

Upon returning home that night, he told his wife about the incident. Then a few days later, he returned to the site with his wife and daughter. He took some of the strange pieces over to a neighbor Floyd Proctor to show him. The material resembled a piece of aluminum foil, but was a bit thicker. They noticed that as they tried to crumple it in their hands it would not lose its shape. The two men attempted to cut and burn the mysterious material, but to no avail. It was unlike anything they had ever seen before.

"Mac" Brazel   Floyd and Loretta Proctor

He took some of the debris to Roswell Deputy B.A. Clark who contacted the Roswell Army Air Field known as RAAF. On July 7, Major Jesse Marcel, a Counter Intelligence Corps officer of the 509th Composite Group at Roswell, New Mexico and Sheridan Cavitt, Head of the Roswell Army Counter Intelligence Corps came out and inspected the site. The 509th Composite Group (509 CG) was created during WWII. Its task was the deployment of nuclear weapons including the atomic bombing of Hiroshima, Japan in 1945.

Fort Worth Star-Telegram - July 9, 1947
Brig. General Roger Ramey – Fort Worth Army Airfield

Fort Worth Star-Telegraph - July 9, 1947
Brig. General Ramey holding a telegram and DuBose

Fort Worth Star-Telegram Photograph Collection

After their initial inspection, they concluded that it was pieces of a crashed UFO. They gathered up some of the debris and took it back to the base. Once there, they briefed Colonel Blanchard. Shortly afterward, personal were gathered, equipment and resources were deployed, and the area was secured. They discovered debris that had been strewn along a large area measuring three-quarters of a mile long and three hundred feet wide. Colonel Blanchard notified Lieutenant Walter Hunt, the base Public Information Officer advising him that a flying disc had crashed and it was being recovered. Lieutenant Hunt immediately issued a press release.

Roswell Daily Record - July 9, 1947 - Initial Press Release

However, as the newspaper quickly reported the incident, a few hours after the initial press release, Brigadier General Roger Ramey, head of the Eighth Air Force in Fort Worth, TX, issued another press release claiming they had only recovered a weather balloon.

Fort Worth Star Telegram - July 9, 1947

Major Jesse Marcel posing for photos with the "replacement" of remnants of a weather balloon.

Mac Brazel was whisked off to the base to be questioned. Once there, he was told the debris was nothing more than a weather balloon and they strongly encouraged him to recant his story. Strangely enough the newspaper retracted the story the following day.

Harassed Rancher who Located 'Saucer' Sorry He Told About It

W. W. Brazel, 48, Lincoln county rancher living 30 miles south east of Corona, today told his story of finding what the army at first described as a flying disk, but find caused him to doubt that it ever found anything else that it a bomb he sure wasn't going to say anything about it.

Brazel was brought here late yesterday by W. E. Whitmore, of radio station KGFL, had his picture taken and gave an interview to the Record and Jason Kellahin, sent here from the Albuquerque bureau of the Associated Press to cover the story. The picture he posed for was sent out over AP telephoto wire sending machine specially set up in the Record office by R. D. Adair, AP wire chief sent here from Albuquerque for the sole purpose of getting out his picture and that of sheriff George Wilcox, to whom Brazel originally gave the information of his find.

Brazel related that on June 14 he and an 8-year old son, Vernon were about 7 or 8 miles from the ranch house of the J. B. Foster ranch, which he operates, when

they came upon a large area of bright wreckage made up on rubber strips, tinfoil, a rather tough paper and sticks.

At the time Brazel was in a hurry to get his round made and he did not pay much attention to it. But he did remark about what he had seen and on July 4 he, his wife, Vernon and a daughter Betty, age 14, went back to the spot and gathered up quite a bit of the debris.

The next day he first heard about the flying disks, and he wondered if what he had found might be the remnants of one of these.

Monday he came to town to sell some wool and while here he went to see sheriff George Wilcox and "whispered kinda confidential like" that he might have found a flying disk.

Wilcox got in touch with the Roswell Army Air Field and Maj. Jesse A. Marcel and a man in plain clothes accompanied him home, where they picked up the rest of the pieces of the "disk" and went to his home to try to reconstruct it.

According to Brazel they simply

could not reconstruct it at all. They tried to make a kite out of it, but could not do that and could not find any way to put it back together so that it would fit.

Then Major Marcel brought it to Roswell and that was the last he heard of it until the story broke that he had found a flying disk.

Brazel said that he did not see it fall from the sky and did not see it before it was torn up, so he did not know the size or shape it might have been, but he thought it might have been about as large as a table top. The balloon which held it up, if that was how it worked, must have been about 12 feet long, he felt, measuring the distance by the size of the room in which he sat. The rubber was a smoky gray in color and scattered over an area about 200 yards in diameter.

When the debris was gathered up the tinfoil, paper, tape, and sticks made a bundle about three feet long and 7 or 8 inches thick, while the rubber made a bundle about 18 or 20 inches long and about 8 inches thick. In all, he estimated, the entire lot would

have weighed maybe five pounds.

There was no sign of any metal in the area which might have been used for an engine and no sign of any propellers of any kind, although at least one paper fin had been glued onto some of the tinfoil.

There were no words to be found anywhere on the instrument, although there were letters on some of the parts. Considerable scotch tape and some tape with flowers printed upon it had been used in the construction.

No strings or wire were to be found but there were some eyelets in the paper to indicate that some sort of attachment may have been used.

Brazel said that he had previously found two weather observation balloons on the ranch, but that what he found this time did not in any way resemble either of these.

"I am sure what I found was not any weather observation balloon," he said. "But if I find anything else, besides a bomb they are going to have a hard time getting me to say anything about it."

Roswell Daily Record —July 9, 1947

Roswell Army Air Field (RAAF) claimed this was part of a secret military project called Classified Project Mogul. The project was first conceived by Dr. Maurice Ewing of Columbia University in New York. His study of the sound channel in the ocean proved that sound waves generated by explosives could be carried by currents deep within the ocean. He proposed that sound waves may also be transmitted within the sound channel in the upper atmosphere. By

266

employing radar reflectors and sonar equipment attached to a seventy foot long string of high-altitude balloons, the purpose was long distance detection of sound waves generated by Soviet atomic bomb tests. The project was headed by Major Robert T. Crane, Colonel Marcellus Duffy, and Captain Albert C. Trakowski.

The RAAF maintained that what was found that day was the remnants of NYU Flight 4 that was launched earlier on June 4. However, this explanation did not sit well with Brazel for the fact that he and his neighbor could not cut or burn the material. Likewise, it did not satisfy Tommy Tryee, a hired hand on the ranch, who maintained that the sheep would no longer cross the debris field and had to be driven the long way around to water.

The story of the Roswell incident quickly disappeared. However, in its place was born the most massive UFO cover-up the United States Government has ever engaged in. Years later more and more people began to come forward with information. Researchers contend there was more than one crash site. It is believed that the craft may have left debris in one location during the severe thunder storm, but regained altitude again only to finally crash in Corona, New Mexico which is forty-five miles away. Furthermore, according to a secret FBI Memorandum from Guy Hottel of the Strategic

Air Command dated March 22, 1950, there were three crash sites.

Guy Hottel   Memo to FBI – March 29-1950

"An investigator for the Air Force stated that three so-called flying saucers have been recovered in New Mexico. They were described as being circular in shape with raised centers, approximately 50 feet in diameter. Each one was occupied by three bodies of human shape, but only three feet tall, dressed in metallic cloth of a very fine texture. Each body was bandaged in a manner similar to the blackout suits used by speed flyers and fast pilots."

"According to Mr. XXX informant, the saucers were found in New Mexico due to the fact that the Government has a very high-powered radar set-up in that area and it is believed the radar interferes with the controlling mechanics of the saucers."

Many UFO proponents arrest that indeed several alien crafts were found, the occupants were captured, and the military engaged in a massive cover-up. Among the debris was a lightweight shiny tan metallic material that could not be bent, folded, dented, or melted. It was said that even when hit with a sledge hammer, the hammer would just bounce off never leaving a scratch. There are photos of what some speculate to be an I-beam about the length of a pencil. On this beam is a purplish hue inscription that looks very similar to Greek Hieroglyphs: "ELEPHTHERIA" which means liberty.

Plate with mysterious symbols

Drawing by Major Jesse Marcel

Sergeant Melvin E. Brown maintained he was present at the second site guarding the truck containing alien bodies. He also guarded the hanger at Roswell Army Air Field while crates from the site were stored there. Lewis

Rickett an Army Counter-Intelligence Agent or CIC said he assisted with the retrieval of debris from the crash. A nurse who worked at the Roswell Army Air Field explained how she had accidentally walked into an examination room where doctors were bent over the bodies of three creatures. They resembled humans, but had small bodies, spindly arms, and giant heads. Elias Benjamin, an MP at the base, recalled that he guarded aliens on gurneys that had been brought into the Roswell base hospital. One of them was still alive. Glenn Dennis, a former mortician, gave a detailed personal account about how he assisted in alien autopsies at Roswell. Captain Oliver W. Henderson, a member of the First Air Transport Unity at Roswell Army Air Field claimed he was the pilot of the C-54 flight carrying wreckage from Roswell to Wright-Patterson Air Force Base. Norma Gardner, a typist with top security clearance at Wright-Patterson said she typed autopsy reports on alien beings and saw two bodies.

Majestic 12

Adjacent to the Adena burial mounds is Wright-Patterson Air Force Base which was established in 1917. It is the oldest flying field in the world where Wilber and Orville Wright conducted most of their early flight tests. During

Operation Blue Fly it was known for recovering and reverse engineering of foreign government aircraft during WWI. Later, it became part of Project Moon Dust where it was reported that alien crafts were brought to Hangar 18, Area B in order to reverse engineer the technology. Likewise, extraterrestrial beings were placed in deep, climate controlled, underground cryogenic chambers to preserve. 39°49'23N 84°02'58W

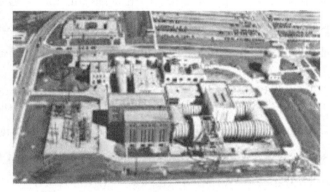

Wright-Patterson Air Force Base, Dayton, Ohio

Project Moon Dust was an operation to recover objects and debris from space vehicles that had survived re-entry from space to Earth. In the following document from Gilbert R. Levy, Chief Counterintelligence Division, he stated, "Moon Dust is a classified nickname for recovery of reported material from space sputnicks."

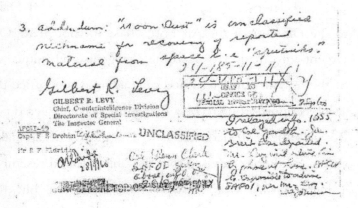

Department of the Air Force Classified Document - Moon Dust

Teletype July, 8, 1947 concerning the Roswell crash

273

Teletype July 8, 1947, 6:17 p.m. from FBI Dallas to the Director of the Air Force Base in Cincinnati, OH: Urgent information concerning flying disc. Headquarters of the 8th Air Force telephonically advised this office that an object purporting to be a flying disc was recovered near Roswell, New Mexico, this day. The disc is hexagonal in shape. Further be advised that the object found resembles a high altitude balloon with radar reflector, but that telephonic conversation between their office and Wright Field had not borne out this belief. Disc is being transported to Wright Field by special plane for examination. Information is provided to this office because of C7 National interest in case and the fact that National Broadcasting Company, Associated Press, and others are attempting to break story of location of disc today. Request Wright Field to advice Cincinnati office results of examination. No further investigation being conducted."

Stanton Friedman is acknowledged as the premier investigator of the Roswell Incident. He was a nuclear physicist who worked for General Electric and Westinghouse to assist with the design and development of fusion rockets and nuclear power plants for space applications. In his book "Crash at Corona," he exposes the government's successful forty year conspiracy to conceal the truth behind America's most documented UFO encounter by way of the "Majestic 12."

An eight page memo dated November, 18, 1952, outlined the establishment of a secret group "the Majestic 12" by outgoing President Harry Truman. The memo was prepared for the new President-elect Dwight D. Eisenhower. The document describes the fact that the United States government did indeed recover three crashed alien spacecraft and bodies in New Mexico. Two were located immediately in 1947 and the third was discovered in 1949 in Horse Mesa west of Magdalena. Because all the crafts were exactly alike, it is believed the one at Horse Mesa crashed at the same time in 1947. However because of the remoteness of the area, the craft was not located until a rancher had discovered it on his property.

The sole purpose was to determine how to handle the implications of the Roswell incident and the existence of extraterrestrial beings. The documents were received on a roll of undeveloped 35mm black and white film to Hollywood movie producer and UFO researcher Jaime Shandera in 1984. There was no note in the package or a return address. The only clue was the postmark that indicated it came from Albuquerque, New Mexico. He had earlier worked with a group of military intelligence personal who referred to themselves as the "Insiders" who expressed a desire to have the true facts released to the public. The documents were handed over to the FBI that spent over a year investigating it. They concluded that if they were forged, the details of people and events were quite accurate and coincided with their internal documents. If they were real, they could not get the U.S. Government to acknowledge that they had lost them. In 1994, Don Berliner, a long time UFO researcher and independent journalist also received a roll of film containing 23 more pages dated April 1954. It was a detailed instruction manual entitled "Extraterrestrial Entities and Technology, Recovery, and Disposal."

Majestic 12 - Instruction Manual

TOP SECRET
EYES ONLY
THE WHITE HOUSE
WASHINGTON

September 24, 1947.

MEMORANDUM FOR THE SECRETARY OF DEFENSE

Dear Secretary Forrestal:

As per our recent conversation on this matter,
you are hereby authorized to proceed with all due
speed and caution upon your undertaking. Hereafter
this matter shall be referred to only as Operation
Majestic Twelve.

It continues to be my feeling that any future
considerations relative to the ultimate disposition
of this matter should rest solely with the Office
of the President following appropriate discussions
with yourself, Dr. Bush and the Director of Central
Intelligence.

Letter from President Harry Truman
to Majestic 12 – September 24, 1947

MAJESTIC 12

1. Almirante Roscoe H. Hillenkoetter
2. Dr. Vannevar Bush
3. Secretario James V. Forrestal
4. General Nothan Twining
5. General Hoyt S. Vanderberg
6. Dr. Detlev Bronk
7. Dr. Jerome Hunsaker
8. Almirante Sidney W. Souers
9. Mr. Gordon Gray
10. Dr. Donal Menzel
11. General Robert M. Montague
12. Dr. Lloyd V. Berkener

Majestic 12

General Nathan Twining: Chairman of the Joint Chiefs of Staff and Commander of the Air Material Command based at Wright-Patterson Air Base where the debris and bodies from the Roswell crash were taken. He was known to have cancelled a scheduled trip on July 8, 1947, just after the crash at Roswell and the same day Roswell Army Base sent out a press release stating that a flying saucer had been recovered. In a now infamous memo, he stated that UFOs are real.

James Farrestal: Secretary of the Navy, first Secretary of Defense in 1947 during the time of the Roswell crash. In 1949, he mysteriously committed suicide. However, conspiracy theorists believe he was murdered because he didn't want to keep this information secret any longer.

General Robert M. Monteque: Head of the Armed Forces Special Weapons Center and Army General at Fort Bliss who had control over the White Sands Nuclear Facility during the time of the Roswell incident.

Dr. Lloyd V. Berkener: Member of the Joint research and Development Board, Member of the CIA-funded UFO Committee that determined that UFOs did not constitute a threat to the U.S. national security.

Gorden Gray: Secretary of the Army and Consultant on UFOs that reported directly to CIS Director Walter B. Smith.

Dr. Donald Menzel: Director of the Harvard College Observatory and expert in cryptoanalysis, the science of breaking codes and deciphering unknown languages and symbols.

General Hoyt Vandenburg: Chief of Staff of the U.S. Air Force and former Director of Central Intelligence allegedly in charge of security for the MJ-12 Group.

Rear Admiral Roscoe Hillenkoetter: First Director of the CIA and a member of NICAP, the National Investigations Committee on Aerial Phenomena.

Dr. Vannevar Bush: Researcher and Developer at MIT and the Carnegie Institute, Head of the Office of scientific Research and Development which was responsible for the development of the atomic bomb.

Admiral Sidney Soners: First Director of Central Intelligence.

Dr. Detlev Bronk: Physiologist and Aviation Expert.

Dr. Jerome Hunsaker: Head of the National Advisory Committee on Aeronautics.

The first conspiracy book regarding Roswell was "The Roswell Incident" written in 1980 by Charles Berlitz and William Moore. Through interviews with hundreds of credible witnesses and sources, they uncovered an immense amount of pertinent information supporting the theory that alien crafts had been traveling over the desert in New Mexico possibly observing our nuclear weapons activity when longitudinal waves were activated at Roswell's base. These waves capable of traveling at multiples of the speed of light, interfered with the controlling mechanisms of the crafts causing them to malfunction. Moreover, the military went to great lengths to discredit the witnesses and devise a massive cover-up; a cover-up that instead fueled so many to come forward.

The USAP or Unacknowledged Special Access Project is the name given to highly secretive or "Black Budget" Projects. Personnel assigned to such tasks have the highest military clearance. With this comes the understanding that they are sworn, no ordered to secrecy. Should anyone ever inquire about said project, they must reply stating that no such project exists. Answering with "no comment" could imply otherwise. All personnel were required to sign an agreement by the executive order of then president Ronald Reagan to waive their constitutional rights.

With that being said, what happens when a person working such a project becomes a threat or is suspected of breaking the code of silence? Over the years, millions in "bribes" were issued through what is known as TWEP orders or Terminate With Extreme Prejudice. Others were not as fortunate as the government chose instead to refute any statements they had publicly shared.

Sector 4 –S4

About ten miles south from Groom Lake and thirteen miles from the Groom Mine in the Emigrant Valley is the Papoose Mountain Range that borders another dry body of water known as the Papoose Lake. Part of the mountain was previously owned by the Papoose Mining Company and was once the site of the Kelly Mine. Although the claim discovered deposits of gold, silver, and lead, it did not prove to be prosperous enough to continue working the mine. Therefore, the mine was abandoned. Or was it?

There are several roads leading toward the mountains, however it is one particular dirt road that is of great significance. It is said this road with a small turnabout area near the old Kelly Mine leads to a top secret location known as "Sector 4 or S4."

Jan Harzan Executive Director of MUFON claims there is a secret underground facility with nine hangar doors sloped at a sixty degree angle that is built into the base of the Papoose Mountains. With the coordinates Latitude 37.0624254N and Longitude 115.503448W, this is reportedly the site where recovered extraterrestrial crafts and beings are kept hidden away.

Although the government adamantly denies any such place exists, the name S4 Area 51 code name Dark Side of the Moon appears in the MJ12 documents. One such document states: Q-94-109A, September 25, 1996, Clearance: Cosmic-Magic; Papoose Site 4, and Authority: Naval Intelligence Space Command. In addition, several secret projects conducted at the site were mentioned:

Project Aquarius: deals with establishing communication with the EBE, Extraterrestrial Biological Entity, from the Zeta Reticuli star system that are said to be working with our scientists and engineers on various projects.

Project Galileo: deals with the Propulsion System and the role of gravity as the propulsion medium. This is a study of harnessing, amplifying, and lensing gravity. Lensing is the process of mass curving space-time such as what occurs when a craft travels between Earth and other galaxies through an area called dark matter.

Project Looking Glass: deals with the Physics of Seeing the effects of artificially produced gravity wave on time. It focuses on gravity and the control of it supporting the theory of control of Space and Time as the key element.

Another strange element about the 6,129 foot Papoose Mountain is that the top has been leveled to form a plateau. Several buildings and an antenna tower with constant white and red lights can be seen at the coordinates 37.12312N 11.1150432W.

On May, 15, 1989, George Knapp investigative reporter at Las Vegas tv station KLAS interviewed a man calling himself Dennis. With his face obscured from the cameras, he proceeded to speak about when he was allegedly employed from 1988-1989 by U.S. Naval Intelligence at a site known as S4 which was located down a dirt road in the Papoose Mountains that are near Area 51. In November of the same year, he was interviewed again. However this time, he did not hide in a shroud of secrecy and shared his real name Robert Scott Lazar.

Robert Scott Lazar

Bob Lazar claimed that he was part of a secret project known as Project Galileo where he was employed as an engineer to reverse engineer purported extraterrestrial technology. All the systems of the craft were reported to have been operated by an antimatter reactor that was powered by "element 115." Moscovium, a synthetic chemical with the symbol Mc and atomic number 115, is an extremely radioactive element. It was first synthesized in 2003 by a team of Russian and American scientist in Russia at the Joint Institute for Nuclear Research or JINR.

He claimed to have seen nine different extraterrestrial craft at the site. Through reverse engineering, he began working on a space probe that would create its own gravitational pull enabling it to warp space and time.

In 1992, he told his story once again to Art Bell on Coast-to-Coast AM radio. Unfortunately despite his allegations, the government never acknowledged his employment. Theorists believe the government took great measures to attack his authenticity such as having his college records mysteriously expunged.

His coming forward prompted others to do the same as they concurred with his story about the mysterious S4. And yet, it was not without repercussions. Dr. Dan Burisch said he gave 19 years of service to Majestic working on Project Aquarius under Vice Admiral J.M. McConnell former Director of the National Security Agency. However when he wrote the book "Eagles Disobey," his PhD degree mysterious disappeared.

CIA Director William Colby was once a part of Majestic. On April 27, 1996, his body was mysteriously found floating near a sand bar by the Potomac River ... nine days after the area was extensively searched. The coroner quickly determined the cause of death to be drowning.

He had been staying at his cottage that week. Around 7:30, he talked to his wife on the phone stating that he had a busy day, was going to cook dinner, and then turn in for the evening. So why was his canoe found on a sand bar the following day and how did he come up missing? Why was the open bottle of wine still on the table and his computer and radio on? Why was his wallet with all his identification spread all over the table?

Things just didn't add up. When his canoe was discovered not far from his cottage by a local fisherman, it had so much sand inside that it took the man an hour to empty it. He noticed there was a tow rope attached to the front of the canoe. Strangely, there was no sight of a life jacket or paddles. The searchers did an extensive search of the area, but the investigation was only done within 500 meters of his house.

It didn't make sense to the fisherman that Colby would decide to go out in the canoe after the sun had set at 8:00 especially since the wind was up and the water was choppy. The most telling factor was that nine days later his body was discovered by the same sand bar where the canoe was found.

Theorists believe that men came to his cabin, made him empty his pockets so there would be no identification, and forced him into a vehicle. Then two men tied a tow rope to the canoe moving it the secluded sand bar. They drove him to another location and killed him, but concealed the body for nine days hoping it would decompose to the point that identification and cause of death could not be determined. In conclusion, there was no way possible that the body would not have been discovered had it been in the water at the time of the investigation.

Had Colby known too much and was he getting ready to tell it all at the next Congressional meeting? Theorists contend that the government will go to great extremes to eliminate their enemies and even their own.

Chapter 9
Ossippe Triangle

New Hampshire is one of America's thirteen Colonies, deriving its name from the English county of Northamptonshire where Captain John Mason was born. Mason, a sailor, was issued a commission and provided with a ship by King James I in 1620 in order to suppress piracy in Newfoundland. As a reward, he received a patent from the Plymouth Council for New England for all the territory between the Merrimack and Kennebec Rivers. While still in England, he sent two fishing merchants Edward and Thomas Hilton to establish a fishing port. Not all the settlers arriving in New England came seeking religious freedom. Many came to seek their fortune fishing, fur trading, and selling lumber. The mighty old growth of the forests was highly sought after by the English Crown using it for ship masts. In 1629, the area became known as the New Hampshire Colony. Six months before the Declaration of Independence was signed, New Hampshire Colony was the first colony to declare its independence from England.

Ossipee, population 4,400, is a small town in central New Hampshire named after the Ossippe people one of the twelve Algonquian tribes. The town shares its name with a mountain range known as the Ossipee Mountains.

One hundred million years ago, in what is now New Hampshire, there was a fracture in the volcano and an eruption forced molten magma to the surface. As the magna emerged, circular sections collapsed into the empty chamber. Ten million years later, a second eruption occurred as more magna was forced up along the edges of the first plug creating a ring dike. The Ossipee Mountains are the remains of that long extinct volcanic vent or ring dike. A dike is a crack in the bedrock which is filled with magma. A ring dike is a circular crack which is caused by a collapse of the magna chamber ceiling underground. Magna erupted through these circular structures creating the mountains. The diameter of this range is about ten miles and the distance around the base is forty miles. It is estimated that the original volcano may have been 10,000 feet tall similar to Mt. Fuji. The highest point in the range is Mt. Shaw which is 2,990 feet. Lake Winnipesaukee which is a glacial lake is 21 miles long, 9 miles wide, covering 69 square miles, 180 feet deep, and contains 258 islands.

The Winnipesaukee whose name means "smile of the Great Spirit" called the lake "beautiful lake in a high place." They considered the mountains a sacred place.

In the midst of all this beauty, is a mysterious place known as The Ossipee Triangle. The coordinates begin north in Franconia, to Tuftonboro in the east, and extends down to Salem in the south, and then back up to Franconia again. Within its boundaries are burial mounds, mysterious stone formations, strange sounds, apparitions, missing people, and UFOs.

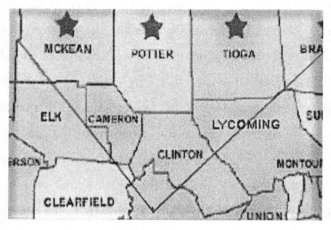

Ossipee Triangle

Mystery Hill

About twenty-five miles inland from the Atlantic Ocean, and near north Salem, in the heart of the woods, is a place known as Mystery Hill. Atop the hill stands a mysterious rock formation that is shrouded in legend. Some call it America's Stonehenge. The site is a 3000 year old megalithic stone formation. Megalithic means "great stone" and describes large stones that have been used to construct a monument without the use of tools or mortar. Covering over thirty acres, it is thought to be the largest and possibly oldest megalithic site in North America.

Mystery Hill

The stones of Mystery Hill were quarried using primitive stone to stone techniques. Who built the site remains a mystery, but carbon dating done by archeologists show there was human occupation in the area as far back as 2000 B.C. Some say the style is the same as that of the ancient Minoan a Bronze Age civilization that lived on the island of Crete. Ogam writing, an Old Norse Runic alphabet, on some of the stone slabs suggests it could possibly be of Viking origin.

The Eye of Bel

One such marking is of "the Eye of Bel." Belenus, one of the most ancient and most widely worshipped of the Celtic deities is a sun god. He was thought to ride the sun across the sky in a horse-drawn chariot. The prefix "Bel" means shining and Beltane meaning "the fire of the god Bel" celebrates the rise of the sun.

Eye of Bel

Although it is referred to as America's Stonehenge, the stones of Stonehenge are quite larger in comparison at up to forty-five tons compared to Mystery Hill's stones with the largest being eleven tons. While Stonehenge is located on a plain and arranged in circles, Mystery Hill is on a hill with stones arranged in various patterns

The stones of Mystery Hill were quarried using primitive stone to stone techniques. Who built the site remains a mystery, but carbon dating done by archeologists indicates there was human occupation in the area as far back as 2995 B.C. Some say the style is the same as that of the ancient Celtic Minoan a Bronze Age civilization that lived on the Isle of Crete. Others contend that it was built by Giants. Ogham writing, an old Norse Runic alphabet, on some of the stone slabs suggests there may have been Viking presence at some point. Nonetheless, artifacts and carvings support the theory that an advanced culture once lived there.

The huge stone formations consist of small stone walls, odd stone arrangements, and thirteen underground chambers. Along the perimeter are several confirmed astronomical alignments. Below on the slopes of the hill is a fourteenth chamber, two natural caves, springs, stone walls, cairns, and standing stones.

The astronomical alignments mark the Midwinter Solstice sunrise and sunset; November 1 sunrise and sunset; Spring and Fall sunrise and sunset; May 1 sunrise and sunset; Midsummer Solstice sunrise and sunset; August 1 sunrise and sunset; True north, aligned to the star Thuban the pole star of 2830 B.C; 200 alignments with the moon, and 45 different stars.

Alignment with the Summer Solstice Sunrise

Thuban is a star seen in the northern hemisphere located near the Big Dipper which was the North Pole star from 4000-2000 B.C. It was closest to the pole in 2830 B.C. The name is derived from an Arabic word meaning "dragon's tail." The two outer stars of the dipper point to the modern day pole star Polaris and the two inner stars Phecda and Megrez point to Thuban.

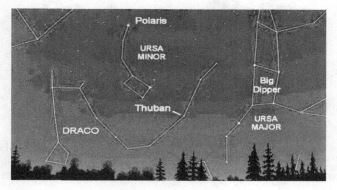

Thuban "Dragon's Tail"

Among the stone formations, is something called the Sacrificial Stone. The stone slab is rectangular, eight feet long, six feet wide, and ten inches thick. Raised up on three columns of stone, it weights over four tons and has a groove scored into its perimeter to collect liquid and drain it off the side. This is similar to altar stones found in megalithic sites in Europe. Was this altar used for water ceremonies? Or perhaps it was used to sacrifice animals or even humans?

Sacrificial Table

Beneath the sacrificial altar is the Oracle Chamber. It is an elaborate web of pathways and carved out places that are thought to have been used during rituals. A 4x6 shaft lined with thin facing stones runs from the exterior and enters through the interior wall. A stone bench is in the chamber and s "Speaking Tube" emerges above ground yet concealed underneath the altar which when spoken through, causes voices to be warped and amplified.

The Oracle Chamber

Archaeologists maintain that only two types of stone shapes were used in construction, triangle and rectangle. They also discovered something remarkable concerning two chambers named Calendar-I and Calendar-II. The doorway of the chamber of Calendar-I was built to face the Equinox sunrise. The chamber's measurements equal a sacred geometry ratio of 1.617; Pi is 1.1618. The chamber of Calendar-II was built oriented to the Winter Solstice. On the morning of December 21, the sun rises in the center of the entrance. The chamber's measurements equal a radio of 2.1 which is the same as the King's Chamber of the Great Pyramid of Giza in Egypt. In addition, the chamber is located over an underground spring and ley line.

Calendar I – Equinox Sun Rise

Calendar II Chamber

"Interrupted Journey"
The Hill Incident

In the southern part of the Triangle, is Ossipee Lake that was carved out by a glacier during the Ice Age. It covers 3,257 acres and is the sixth largest lake in New Hampshire. There are also many ponds that are considered bottomless and may be connected by volcanic vents. It has been said that UFOs have been seen plunging into these deep ponds.

The first recorded UFO photo was taken at the Mt. Washington observatory in 1870. The first widely publicized report of an alien abduction in the United States was the

Betty and Barney Hill Abduction in 1961. It is known as the "Hill Incident" and the "Zeta Reticuli Incident" because the couple reported they had been abducted by aliens who claimed to be from the Zeta Reticili System.

Betty and Barney Hill

The Hills lived in Portsmouth, New Hampshire. Barney worked for the U.S. Postal Service and Betty was a Supervisor for the Child Welfare Department. It was September 19, 1961, at around 10:30 p.m. when they were returning home from a vacation at Niagara Falls. When they were north of Lincoln, New Hampshire on U.S. Route 3, (43°54'131"N 71°39'50"W) Betty noticed a bright light in the sky that she thought was a star. She watched as it began to move below the moon, past the planet Jupiter, and upwards to the west of the moon. Then Betty thought she saw a falling star, but instead of falling, it moved upward. Soon it began to move erratically and grew larger and brighter.

Barney a WWII veteran at first dismissed it as a star, but Betty asked him to stop so they might get a better look at whatever it was. They got out of the car, Betty retrieved her binoculars, and observed an odd shaped craft with multi-colored lights, rows of windows and a flat bottom that was now traveling across the face of the moon. Then just as quickly, it changed direction and began to rapidly descend in their direction.

Intrigued, the couple returned to their car and drive toward Franconia Notch, a major mountain pass through the White Mountains in hopes of getting a closer look. They continued to watch the mysterious craft as it came closer and closer. It was almost as if the object was following them. Betty recalled that it was about forty feet long and appeared to be rotating.

When they were about one mile south of Indian Head, the craft began to rapidly descend toward their car prompting Barney to stop right in the middle of the highway.

About 80-100 feet above them, the huge craft silently hovered. Barney grabbed his pistol, stepped out of the car, and slowly walked closer. As he looked through the binoculars, he saw about ten humanoid figures peering out the windows of the craft that appeared to be watching him. Suddenly, all but one of them moved to the back of the craft leaving one who was still watching and a long structure descended from beneath the craft.

Frightened, Barney quickly got back into the car and told Betty they needed to get out of there now. As he attempted to drive away, the craft changed directions again hovering directly over their car. They heard a series of beeping sounds, a tingling sensation surged through their bodies, and their minds became clouded. Then they heard a second series of beeping sounds and found themselves thirty-five miles down the road. They had no recollection of driving there and realized they had lost two hours of time.

Upon returning home, the couple both agreed that they had weird sensations running through their bodies. Their watches had quit running and never worked again. Barney noticed the leather strap on his binoculars was torn. Betty remarked that her dress was torn at the hem and zipper. The next morning they observed shiny concentric circles on the truck of the car. Barney took a compass and discovered that if he moved it close to the circles the needle would whirl rapidly. If he moved it away, the needle remained still.

On September 21, Betty decided to report the incident to Major Paul W. Henderson of the Pease Air Force Base. After listening to her account, he compiled Report 100-1-61 and marked it "insufficient data."

Project Blue Book File 100-1-61
The Hill Incident - September 20, 1961

He then forwarded the report to Project Blue Book which was a study of unidentified flying objects conducted by the U.S. Air Force that began in 1952. The project ended in 1970, but not before it collected 12,618 UFO reports.

The couple was never the same after that night. They experienced dreams that they couldn't explain. They were compelled to take repeated showers as if they needed to wash something off that was attached to them somehow. Barney was filled with anxiety and developed an ulcer. Betty began reading every book she could locate about unidentified flying objects and finally decided that they needed to seek assistance in order to make some sense of it all.

She discovered s book written by Marine Corp Major Donald E. Keyhole who was the head of NICAP, National Investigations Committee On Aerial Phenomena. On September 26, she wrote to him relating their story in its entirety. Her letter was in turn passed to Walter N. Webb.

Betty Hill's letter to Major Keyhoe
September 16, 1961

Betty contacted Dr. Benjamin Simon a respected psychiatrist and neurologist. On January 4, 1964, the Hills allowed him to do some hypnotic regression sessions, a treatment to unlock suppressed memories, to enable them to recall the details of the missing two hours. Simon conducted separate sessions with each of them and found their stories were very similar. Barney recalled how a grey being about five feet tall put him on a small rectangular table, did a physical examination, and counted his vertebrae. He didn't see the being's mouth move as they communicated. They communicated through thought transference or telepathy and there was no language barrier. He remembered the large eyes. He said, "Those eyes. They're in my brain."

Betty recalled a very similar encounter with the beings. In addition, they inserted a long needle about six inches into her stomach. When she asked where they had come from, one of the beings showed her. Later, Betty drew a map depicting twelve stars, two of which were brighter, connected by lines and thirteen lesser stars that formed distinctive groups. She said the stars connected by lines were "trade routes." This drawing of a star formation is eerily similar to the Zeta Reticili System in the Milky Way. Three of the stars in the cluster were unknown until 1969; no astronomer knew their position in 1963. Yet, Betty was able to draw a map of these stars in 1963.

**Barney Hill's drawing during hypnosis
of the being he saw on the craft**

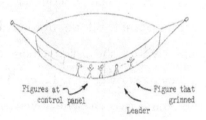

Figures at
control panel

Leader

Figure that
grinned

Barney Hill's drawing of the craft in the sky

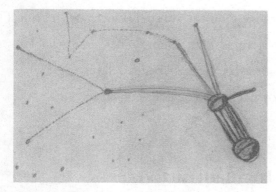

Betty Hill's drawing of the star system
that the being showed her they were from

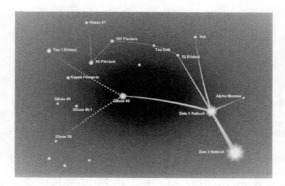

Zeta Reticili System in the Milky Way
At the time this system was unknown to us

The Zeta Reticili is a wide binary star system consisting of two main stars, Zeta 1 and Zeta 2 that are orbiting around their common center. Zeta is slightly smaller, cooler and more orange than the sun while Zeta 2 is identical to the sun. The system is 220 trillion miles and 39.3 light years from the Earth. Some believe this is where extraterrestrials known as Greys reside.

Incident at Exeter

Another one of the best documented and widely publicized accounts in UFO history occurred on September 3, 1965, in Kensington, New Hampshire about five miles south of Exeter. It became known as the "Incident at Exeter."

Around 2:00 a.m. eighteen year old Norman Muscarello had just left the residence of his girlfriend who lived in Amesbury, Massachusetts. Because he had no vehicle he was inclined to attempt to hitch a ride the eight miles back to his home. The only problem was that with it being so late there was almost no traffic on the highway that night. As he continued along Highway 150, he observed lights in the sky coming from the north and heading in a southerly direction.

Then he noticed a series of five flashing lights in the nearby woods. They were so bright that they illuminated the woods and a farmhouse owned by the Dinings.

The lights began to approach in his direction. His survival instinct warned him to take cover so he began to run across the road, but having somehow tripped in the process he found himself in a ditch. The lights changed direction and hovered over the farmhouse before retreating into the woods again.

Luckily for Norman, just then a car came along. He frantically waved the vehicle down and they stopped. He asked the driver if he would take him to the police station in Exeter and he complied.

Upon arriving at the station around 2:24 a.m., he was relieved to see his friend Officer Reginald Toland and related his story to him. Officer Toland radioed Officer Bertrand Jr. who had strangely enough at 12:30 a.m. had a similar conversation with a woman on Highway 108. He had come upon a distressed woman who was sitting in her car along the side of the highway. She began to tell him how a huge object with flashing red lights had been following her for twelve miles, hovered overhead for a while, and then flew away. He didn't quite believe the story, but still sat with the woman about 15 minutes until she felt able to drive home. Now upon hearing a very similar account from Norman, he decided to drive back to the location with him to investigate.

As they walked toward the woods, they heard the sound of frantic horses kicking their stalls in a nearby corral and the dogs began howling. They observed an object with red flashing lights, which Officer Bertrand described as being almost the size of a barn rise up from the woods that were just beyond the correl. The object began to move closer to them in a rocking motion.

The two men ran back to the patrol car where Officer Bertrand radioed Officer David Hunt for assistance. While they waited for his arrival, they continued to observe the mysterious craft as it hovered 100 feet away from them at an altitude of about 100 feet. The craft maintained a rocking motion while pulsating red lights flashed in rapid sequence; first from right to left 5-4-3-2-1, then left to right 1-2-3-4-5.

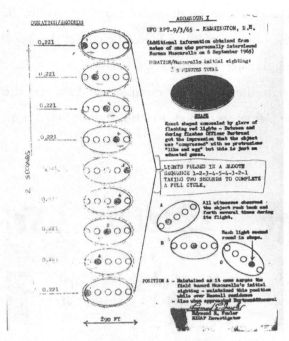

September 3, 1965 - UFO Report
Drawing by Officer Bertrand
Raymond R. Fowler - NICAP Investigator

Norman Muscarello, David Hunt,
Eugene Bertrand, and Reginald Toland
Union Leader Newspaper

When Officer Hunt arrived at the scene, he also observed the object until it suddenly flew over the woods and disappeared. Earlier he had seen a B-47 fly overhead and remarked that there was no comparison between the two. The officers then returned to the station to report their findings.

September 5, 1965 - The Exeter News

Their report was dispatched to Pease Air Force Base and Major David Griffin and Lieutenant Alan Brandt were sent to interview the men. Afterward they asked them not to relay their sightings top the press. However, a reporter from the Manchester Union Leader newspaper had already interviewed them before hand.

Pease Air Force Base declared that there had been five B-74s in the air at the time as part of Operation Big Blast. Major Griffin sent his report to Project Blue Book stating that despite the credibility of the witnesses, he reviewed the area and found no evidence for probable cause. The conclusion of the report stated "A/C from Operation Big Blast and observations of the stars and planets." Later, the Pentagon informed the press that the men had only observed a high-altitude Strategic Air Command exercise. Also, a "weather inversion" had taken place where a layer of cold air becomes trapped between warm layers causing a natural phenomena making stars and planets to appear twinkling.

Pentagon Doesn't Believe UFO Exeter Sightings

WASHINGTON, D.C. — The Pentagon believes that, after intensive investigation, it has come up with a natural explanation of the UFO sightings in Exeter, N.H., on Sept. 3.

A spokesman said the several reports stemmed from "multiple objects in the area," by which they mean a high-altitude Strategic Air Command exercise out of Westover Mass, was going on at the time in the area.

A second important factor was what is called a "weather inversion" wherein a layer of cold air is trapped between warm layers.

The Pentagon spokesman said this natural phenomena causes "stars and planets to dance and twinkle."

The spokesman said "We believe what the people saw that night was stars and planets in unusual formations."

In other words, the Pentagon doesn't believe the Exeter sightings were of men, or something, in flying saucers from outer space.

Washington Post - September 5, 1965

313

PROJECT 10073 RECORD	
1. DATE - TIME GROUP 2-3 Sep 65	2. LOCATION Exeter, N Hampshire
3. SOURCE civilian	10. CONCLUSION 1. A/C from Operation "BIG BLAST" 2. Astro (Stars/Planets)
4. NUMBER OF OBJECTS multiple	
5. LENGTH OF OBSERVATION 2 hr period	11. BRIEF SUMMARY AND ANALYSIS See Case file.
6. TYPE OF OBSERVATION gd visual	Operation "BIG BLAST" in effect in area between 03/0500Z and 03/0600Z.
7. COURSE varied, stationary	Additional observations of Stars/Planets. CAPELLA, JUPITER, and BETELGEUX.
8. PHOTOS ☐ Yes ☒ No	
9. PHYSICAL EVIDENCE ☐ Yes ☒ No	

FORM
FTD SEP 63 0-329 (TDE) Previous editions of this form may be used.

September 3, 1965 - Project 10073 Record
Major Griffin - Pease Air Force Base

Still, the witnesses maintained that what they observed was something not of this world. It was also discovered that the incident occurred an hour after Operation Big Blast was said to have ended so there would not have been any B-47s in the night sky. Furthermore, in the following three weeks after the encounter, there were sixty more reported UFO sightings around Exeter. In 1966, John G. Fuller a journalist for the Saturday Review Magazine published an account of his own investigation into the case of which he claimed to have had his own UFO sighting called "Incident at Exeter."

The Condon Committee

The events were so well founded that the case was brought before a Congressional hearing on April 5, 1966. Air Force Secretary Harold Brown defended the Air Force's part in extraterrestrial studies and Dr. J. Allen Hynek recommended a civilian panel consisting of scientists. After lengthy discussion, it was decided further investigation was warranted. This led to the creation of the University of Colorado UFO Project known as the Condon Committee whose official title was Scientific Study of Unidentified Objects.

On October 6, 1966, the Condon Committee, contract #44620-67-C-0035 with the United States Air Force began with an operating budget of $500,000. The committee was directed by Dr. Edward Uuler Condon, physicist at the University of Colorado; with Franklin E. Roach, astronomer, and Dr. David R. Saunders, member of the university's psychology faculty as co-principal investigators; other members included William K. Hartmann, astronomer; Dr. Frederick Ayer, physicist, and Michael Wertheimer, psychologist.

Dr. Edward Uhler Condon

After examining hundreds of UFO Files from Project Blue Book, the National Investigations Committee on Aerial Phenomena (NICAP), and the Aerial Phenomena Research Organization (APRO), and conducting several on site investigations, the committee came to the conclusion that the study of unidentified flying objects was very unlikely to yield any significant scientific discoveries. They concluded that the twenty-one year study of UFOs had never contributed anything to scientific knowledge. They also recommended there not be a government program to investigate UFO reports. This prompted the Air Force to close Project Blue Book on December 17, 1969, after seventeen years.

Although the Condon Report released in January 1969 was well received by the scientific community, the

American Institute of Aeronautics and Astronautics did not agree and felt future investigation was warranted. It is believed that the downfall of the committee was twofold: the individuals lacked expertise on the subject matter and members usually worked individually instead of a team. Dr. J. Allen Hynek contended that the Condon Report did not arrive at an acceptable conclusion. Many individual reports remained unanswered and the study appeared to be one-sided. The probable cause being they did not understand the nature and scope of what had been presented to them.

Other disturbing events occurred during the study. In January 1967, during a lecture, Dr. Condon stated that the government should not be studying extraterrestrials because the subject was complete nonsense. He was quoted as saying, "But I'm not supposed to reach that conclusion for another year." In July 1967, James Edward McDonald, senior physicist at the Institute for Atmospheric Physics received information from a committee member concerning a memo Robert Low had written on August 9, 1996.

In this memo, he assured two University of Colorado administrators that they could expect the study to conclude that UFO observations had no basis in reality. McDonald found a copy of the memo and sent it to Edward Condon who insisted that since he had no prior knowledge of this

317

memo, it had no bearing on the project's conclusion. Upon hearing of this memo, on April 30, 1968, NICAP severed its ties with the committee.

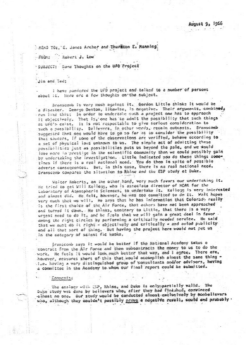

August 9, 1996 Memo written by Robert Lowe

"The simple act of admitting these possibilities puts us beyond pale, and we would lose more in prestige in the scientific community than we could possibly by undertaking the investigation."

With the conclusion of the Condon Report, Walt Andrus member of the APRO management reacted by reinforcing his approach in the UFO investigation field. He maintained that the only way to be proactive was to have a knowledgeable team ready and able to immediately respond when a report came in. Walt convened a meeting with several active UFO investigators in his surrounding area including Illinois, Wisconsin, Missouri, and Kansas in the interest of improving and correlating reports. Dr. Allen Utke, Associate Professor of Chemistry at Wisconsin State University and consultant for APRO proposed an organization that would include all these states. It was agreed upon and the Midwest UFO Network was established in Walt's home town of Quincy, Illinois, with Dr. Utke as its first Director.

In 1970, Dr. Utke stepped down and Walt Andrus became Director. Under his leadership individuals from around the world began to recognize the great potential of the organization. Since this was now more mutual than a Midwest project, the organization's name was changed to Mutual UFO Network or MUFON.

Dr. Allen Utke   Walt Andrus

The Edge of Enigma

There are mysterious doorways, parallel dimensions, and alternate realms in the universe that might compel us to question everything we thought we knew.

There are moments that defy all logic; moments that ooze with intrigue of mysterious beasts, haunting specters, lapses in time, missing people, and bizarre legends.

Even though one might be inherently apprehensive of the unknown, the mere aura of these phenomena lures them in. For others it may involve their thirst for adventure, or a basis to attempt to convince themselves that what they already know isn't real.

"I want to stand as close to the edge as I can without going over. Out on the edge you see all kinds of things you can't see from the center."

Kurt Vonnegut

Made in the USA
Columbia, SC
13 August 2024

39945766R00176